Early American

FURNITURE

Early American
FURNITURE

Designs in the Colonial Style

JAMES M. O'NEILL

Head, Industrial Arts and Fine Arts Department

Baldwin High School; Baldwin, Long Island, New York

McKNIGHT & McKNIGHT PUBLISHING COMPANY

Bloomington, Illinois

Copyright 1963
by McKnight & McKnight Publishing Company

All rights reserved. No part of this book may be reproduced
in any form, without permission in writing from the publishers.

LITHOGRAPHED IN U.S.A.

TO CONNIE . . .

A Most Patient and Understanding "Co-Author"

Preface

AMERICA'S HISTORY is a heritage of accomplishments in many fields of endeavor that should make every American proud. The beauty found in early American craftsmanship has been passed on to us in many forms in our everyday living. Much of this can be seen in various reproductions of the early American and Colonial furniture used in the days of our forefathers.

For those whose interests lie beyond seeing reproductions in magazines, books, and furniture stores, nothing compares with studying the actual pieces found in such historic shrines as Williamsburg, Virginia; Sturbridge Village, Massachusetts; or Winterthur, Delaware. There are also many other collections of excellent caliber.

America's early days saw three general periods of time and furniture:

    Pilgrim   1620-1720
    Colonial   1720-1780
    Federal   1780-1830

Most pieces shown here would be placed in the early Colonial Period, with some in the late Pilgrim Period.

The present day surge of interest in this particular style of furniture is reflected in the work of hundreds of professional cabinet making shops. For the home craftsman and for students, this style lends itself to an ease of construction for a variety of reasons.

The furniture described on the following pages is especially selected for the abilities of students in a high school general woodworking class or of second-year students in a class such as cabinetmaking. Some simplification has helped in making this possible.

The author's students in both of these classes have made the pieces shown in this book. Some have completed other pieces more difficult than those shown here. Thus the difficulty of construction for any of these pieces should be well within the capabilities of any average, interested high school student with normal initiative, a helpful teacher, and usual shop facilities.

The pieces selected have enjoyed outstanding popularity with the students who have made them, as well as with people who are lovers of Early American furniture styles.

It is hoped you may share in this attraction and will successfully complete some of the pieces shown in this book.

I would like to thank

Mr. Alex McKinney, a friend

as well as the most talented craftsman I have known,

for his outstanding, unselfish assistance

in ever so many ways.

J.M.O.

Table of Contents

Preface 7

Introduction 11

MATERIALS AND PROCEDURES OF CONSTRUCTION

1. Working with Pine 15
   Varieties, 15. Dimensions, 15. Avoiding Warped Lumber, 16. Controlling Warpage, 17.

2. Gluing and Clamping 19
   Recommended Glue, 19. Curing Time, 19. Gluing Techniques, 20.

3. Finishing 21
   Finishing Reproductions, 21. Finishing Time, 21. Moisture Problems, 21. Finishing Options, 22. Sprayed Lacquer Finishing Procedure, 22. Alternate Finishing Schedule Using Shellac, 25.

4. Hardware 27

5. Construction Techniques 29
   Plate I, Shrinkage Problems, 30. Plate II, Fastening Tops, 31. Plate III, Raised Panel Doors, 32. Plate IV, Drawer Construction, 33. Plate V, Special Cuts, 34. Plate VI, Construction Details, 35. Plate VII, Gluing Problems, 36.

6. Suppliers 37

7. Important Historical Collections of Early American Furniture ... 39

Table of Contents

SELECTED PIECES OF FURNITURE

1. Foot Stool 42
2. Cranberry Picker Magazine Rack 46
3. Wall Spoon Rack 50
4. Magazine Rack 54
5. Gear Coffee Table 58
6. Bellows Coffee Table 62
7. Butter Churn Table 66
8. Pedestal Table 70
9. Apothecary Chest 74
10. Telephone Night Table 78
11. Colonial Corner Table 82
12. Tiled Coffee Table 86
13. Step End Table 90
14. Towel Bar Table 94
15. Towel Bar Cabinet 98
16. Deacons' Bench 102
17. Hutch Table 106
18. Night Table 110
19. Tripod Table 114
20. Drop Leaf Rudder Table 118
21. Dough Box End Table 122
22. Dry Sink 126
23. Dry Sink Hutch 130
24. Hutch 135

Introduction

ALL DRAWINGS are exploded to better visualize the construction of the furniture. The notes indicated on the drawings cover most of the general construction details. A brief explanation with each drawing gives additional suggestions.

The abbreviations "FHWS" or "FHB" on all drawings represents flat head wood-screws (bright steel). These and brads are used in all pieces.

An important technique is that of rounding and softening various edges, or arrises, on all pieces of furniture for the worn, "colonial look." Some of these arrises will be softened gently, as on the tripod table. Some such as the bellows coffee table, and especially the legs, need a very rugged, worn look.

This worn effect can be made with a cabinet rasp, wood file, or coarse garnet paper. The rasp is a quick way to bring about the worn look, but take care where it is used. The best effect is made by long, even strokes with the rasp or file. For example: the front edge of the main center piece of the hutch (and both shelves) would be "worn" not just for a span of two or three inches, but rather for about three-fourths of the overall length. There should be a deeper center dip for about ten inches where there would have been more wear.

The numbers shown on all drawings indicate a particular part and the letters indicate hardware.

Drawer construction is not shown on the drawings, *nor is the stock for the drawers indicated in the bill of materials.* Refer to Plate IV for drawer construction details and general dimensions. Begin by cutting the drawer front $\frac{1}{32}''$ less than the actual drawer opening. The finish sanding will bring the size of the drawer to an accurate fit.

Do not glue (screw only) the drawer runner and support blocks in place because possible contraction and expansion of the sides or frame may cause the drawer to bind. The lack of glue allows for adjustment if necessary.

Do not glue the drawer bottom into the dados. Glue blocks are optional. They prevent the drawer bottom from rattling. No. 18 gauge brads are used predominently throughout. This is because they will leave smaller holes after being set and can be easily hidden by *distress marks* — see step two of the lacquer finishing procedure in Section 3.

Materials and Procedures of Construction

SECTION 1

Working with Pine

PINE HAS BEEN one of the most popular woods since early colonial days, and for good reasons. It cuts and planes well because of its softness and smooth texture, yet it is firm enough to wear well and take a warm, satisfactory finish. It resists splitting; it is light in weight and easily handled; it is commonly available and thus economical. These characteristics make it an ideal wood for the student, hobbyist, or home craftsman.

VARIETIES

The pine used in colonial days generally was one of three species: *eastern white pine* and two common hard pines, *pitch* (yellow) *pine* and *red pine*. The eastern white pine was the most important forest tree in North America until about 1890 and was widely favored for home furnishings. This soft pine grows from Minnesota to Maine, northward into Canada and southward to the mountains of Georgia. Typical uses of the hard pines were for floorboards, chest lids and heavy tavern tables. They grow in more restricted areas of the East, particularly in the southern Appalachians.

The pieces of furniture illustrated in this book were made from eastern white pine grown in Maine and New Hampshire. This wood is particularly knotty and gives authentic characteristics.

In areas of the country where eastern white pine is not available, there are equally good choices for this furniture style. For example, the excellent and very similar *western white pine* is found in abundance from British Columbia to California, and eastward into Montana. Regardless of geographic location, suitable pine can usually be found at better lumber dealers.

The soft pines make excellent glue joints, and are easily worked and finished. Knots that would be undesirable in many pieces of furniture become an important asset to the style shown here. The proper placement and finishing of these knots add greatly to the attactiveness of the furniture.

DIMENSIONS

Notice the thickness of the wood used in this furniture. An important aspect of this style of furniture is its strong, rugged appearance. Usually this cannot be obtained with common one-inch stock that has been dressed to about three-fourths of an inch, as found in most lumber yards. The alternative for those who cannot obtain the heavier sizes is to build up the necessary thickness by lamination or by edgings. This is not to say that these plans cannot be altered to use three-quarter stock. At times laminating is undesirable because the glue line or the difference in grain structure would detract. Examples where the rugged look is important are the bellows coffee table and the deacons' bench. There are some other cases where three-quarter inch stock could be used and still retain adequate proportions.

Dimensions given on all drawings and on the bills of materials are the actual finished thickness. Lumber is often designated by the rough sawn thicknesses. The following table may be of value when ordering from a lumber yard. In general, it is best to avoid using pine that is wider than 6" or 8" although 10" is occasionally used.

Nominal or Rough Thickness	Actual or Finished Thickness
3"	2 3/4"
2 1/2"	2 3/8"
2"	1 3/4"
1 1/2"	1 3/8"
1 1/4"	1 1/8"
1"	3/4"

AVOIDING WARPED LUMBER

Probably the worst enemy of creating a fine piece of furniture is the problem of warpage. It can vary in different geographic areas, the time of the year, and the kind of wood being used to mention only a few contributing factors.

Pine has many qualities which resist warpage, but unfortunately there can still be problems.

Many causes of warpage can be avoided by a few simple precautions when buying and handling lumber:

1. Know your lumber dealer and his reputation for selling quality lumber, especially among professional cabinetmaking shops. If the dealer is not known, at least pick out your lumber and see what you are buying.
2. Do not have lumber delivered on a rainy day. A responsible dealer should not have to be told this.
3. Storing lumber in over-heated areas can dry the lumber too fast. The heating of modern homes is one of the chief reasons for warping today that didn't occur in colonial times. Modern heating systems cause a wide range of humidity differences that can cause problems with furniture.
4. Never place lumber on or near a damp floor area. For example,

a ground level concrete floor may seem dry, but usually there is enough dampness to cause expansion of the wood on the underside.
5. Do not lean boards against a wall. This causes their own weight to develop a bow in the wood.
6. Lumber should be stacked horizontally or vertically with spacers separating the wood evenly to prevent sagging or bending.
7. Horizontal storage of odd sized pieces should have the longest and widest lumber on the bottom. The pile then forms a stepped pyramid with the short narrow pieces on top.

CONTROLLING WARPAGE

Fig. 1 shows that boards tend to warp opposite the curvature of the annual rings. Plate VII, Fig. 5 shows how to minimize this warpage by alternating the direction of these rings. Warping also occurs when one side of wood absorbs more moisture than the other. A number of construction techniques and features of furniture design control these undesirable tendencies of solid wood.

Some of the various techniques to minimize warpage in furniture are as follows:
1. When gluing up wide panels, alternate the direction of the annual rings as shown in Plate VII, Fig. 5.
2. Drop leaves (see rudder table) may sometimes warp and cause the rule joint to bind. To relieve this warpage, cuts or kerfs on the back side in the direction of the grain, can be made as shown in Plate VI, Fig. 3. This same method can be applied to any surface that is warped as long as the cuts are not visible.
3. Cleats may be used to pull a surface into line. See the lid of the butter churn as an example.
4. Applying stain, wash coat, and seal without proper drying time, or on a humid day can cause wood to hold excess moisture content and create warpage. See Section 3 on finishing.

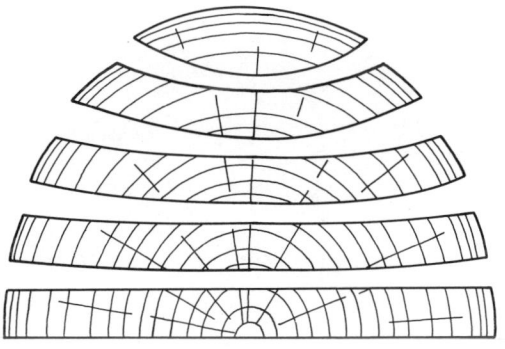

Fig. 1. Direction of Warping

5. Apply similar finishing coats to both sides (top and bottom, front and back) of a flat surface. If a table top has three coats of finish but the underside has none, the bottom will absorb moisture faster and thus cause warpage.
6. Don't wipe the "squeeze out" of glue with a wet rag, as this dampens the exterior of wood causing it to swell.

Other techniques of combating the effects of humidity changes will be found in later sections on gluing, finishing, construction techniques and in details of the various plans. Keep in mind that solid wood is constantly expanding and contracting across the grain and construction details must allow for this movement. Likewise, remember that broad solid surfaces will tend to be warped by moisture changes, and steps must be taken to keep them flat.

SECTION 2

Gluing and Clamping

GLUING AND CLAMPING is one of the important phases of furniture making. Poor work here can cause a great loss of time and effort when glue joints give way and sections have to be torn apart and rebuilt. Certain types of mistakes in joinery can be corrected in the early stages of work, but when gluing errors show up at the completion of the piece the results can be disastrous.

RECOMMENDED GLUE

The selection of the type of glue to use is important. The dirty, hot glue pot often has been replaced in schools and home shops by modern adhesives which are easier to use. Todays workers have a wide variety of adhesives from which to select — each with specific advantages and disadvantages.

Polyvinyl - resin emulsion glue is the type handiest to use for this type of construction. It is ready for use at all times, and one of the most popular dispensers is the plastic "squeeze bottle." This *white glue* is usually sold in pints, quarts, and gallons. It is recommended for constructing the furniture shown in this book.

CURING TIME

Polyvinyl glue sets up quickly and is then colorless. It has strong holding power except when exposed to heat or humidity. It does not cure by a chemical reaction as do some glues, but sets by losing water to the wood and then remains somewhat plastic. The joints may require a clamping time of only one or two hours. However, it is better to wait as long as eight to ten hours, especially on large panels. The rush to unclamp these larger pieces is not worth the remaking of the joint at a later date. Small joints with little or no stress usually can be glued safely in an hour or two.

When insufficient time is allowed for the glue to set, subsequent coats of lacquer have been known to soften the glue joint. This is more likely to happen when the furniture is being produced very quickly. This is not likely in schools or small cabinet shops where such speed of production is unusual.

GLUING TECHNIQUES

Following are some suggestions for improving gluing techniques:

1. Assemble all clamps and materials needed before spreading any glue.
2. "Dry clamp" all pieces to check the tightness of the joint. It must close throughout with minimum pressure.
3. Apply glue to both surfaces being joined, but be careful not to spread too much glue. An excess will not guarantee a strong joint. Allow glue to become tacky, usually this takes about three minutes. Be careful of *starving* a glue joint. This occurs when there is too little glue in the finished joint. Uusually a starved joint is not caused by too little glue being spread although this can be a reason. More commonly it is caused by applying too much pressure or clamping while the glue is too fluid or thin. This is the purpose for allowing the glue to become tacky before clamping. Starved joints can also be caused by wood that contains excessive moisture when glued.

    Normal care in gluing should eliminate any difficulty. A poor glue joint is rare when using white glue with soft pine.
4. When using bar clamps, place them about ten inches apart and apply moderate pressure. Put alternate clamps on opposite sides to maintain even pressure. This prevents "cupping" the panel, which can occur when all clamps are on one side only.
5. Use cauls (1" x 2" hardwood is typical) on the ends of panels to prevent buckling. Clamp with wooden hand screws or C-clamps.
6. Do not wipe the excess glue from the joint with a wet or even damp rag. This only swells the cells of the wood and spreads the glue over a wider area. Leave the beads of excess glue to dry and then scrape and sand them away.
7. Do not apply glue where "squeeze out" could mar a surface that is hard to clean. See Plate VII, Fig. 4.
8. Certain parts should not be glued. Some of these are drawer bottoms, (within dado cuts), raised panel doors (within door frames), and tops of certain tables. See Plates II, III, and IV.
9. Gluing in certain areas can prevent free shrinkage that is of the utmost importance. Failure to allow for this powerful force can cause splitting, opening of joints, and warping. See Plate I.
10. Glue can cause staining. It fills the pores of the wood so they will not stain well, and must be removed thoroughly by sanding. There is nothing more distracting than "back-tracking" to remove glue smears after the piece has been stained for finishing.

SECTION 3
Finishing

CERTAIN BASIC TECHNIQUES must be followed in applying a finish to furniture and these cannot be changed. However, there are numerous variations and a wide range of personal preferences. Probably no other area of furniture construction has so many different ways to accomplish the same end result.

FINISHING REPRODUCTIONS

Modern techniques and materials can create excellent *reproduction finishes* which are more durable and beautiful than were *usually* carried out by our colonial forefathers. Although many pieces did have a high quality finish, these were the exception rather than the rule in early colonial days.

The finishing procedure presented here has been used extensively by the author in his classes. It has been also used by some of the finest craftsmen in the colonial reproduction furniture business, and has met with popular approval by the purchasers of such furniture.

FINISHING TIME

As with practically all finishing methods, short cuts to save time can be made. They can also be costly. *Time* for proper drying is one of the most important factors in good finishing. Cutting drying time can mean a loss of many hours of construction work and the additional unnecessary work of *refinishing*.

MOISTURE PROBLEMS

Moisture is the enemy of both wood and finishing so must be considered at all times. Ideally, low humidity is obviously the best condition for finishing. The range of 20 to 30 per cent relative humidity can be considered excellent. Unfortunately, the air is not often this dry in many places. However, in arid regions 30 per cent relative humidity might be considered unusually high.

Many of the problems of temperature and humidity are solved by large companies through the use of rooms where temperature and humidity are controlled. These conditions do not usually exist in smaller shops and many times risks are taken that can cause trouble. Staining and then wash coating within two hours on a day when the relative humidity is 85 per cent and doing this without the benefit of heat lamps is an example. Obviously this is not allowed in better cabinetmaking shops.

FINISHING OPTIONS

The following finishing procedure is the one used for all furniture illustrated in this book. An alternate procedure using shellac is included for those who desire a quick, easy, but acceptable finish.

The basic procedure suggests a sprayed application. The author believes that once spray equipment has been used, the craftsman will not want to pick up a brush again. This is the opinion of many cabinetmakers.

But many do not have access to spray equipment and it is quite possible to carry out the finishing schedule with a brush. A brushing lacquer should then be substituted for the spraying lacquer specified.

SPRAYED LACQUER FINISHING PROCEDURE

1. FINAL SANDING

Use 6/0 garnet finishing paper.

2. DISTRESSING (SURFACE MARKS)

This operation is unique to colonial furniture construction. It should be first practiced on a scrap piece of similar wood so as to better visualize the final outcome.

Obtain a piece of slag or coke about the size of a closed fist or larger. These can often be found in the ballast of railroad track beds, or around boilers burning coal. There are other possible items for distressing such as crumpled tin can, but they do not have the variety of sharp edges found on slag or coke.

The slag is simply rolled over the surface of the wood. This will leave enough marks for *light distressing* in areas such as the top of the step end table. For distressing to give a look of more *rugged wear*, such as on the bellows coffee table, the wood is struck hard with the slag. For *extreme distressing* some craftsmen use a circular plane (concave cutter) or a block plane ("soften" the corners of the plane iron on a grinder). This can be used on a piece like the cranberry picker magazine rack to create wide and rather deep cuts. However, this must be done carefully or the effect may become ruinous. Practice thoroughly on scrap. Some may consider this to be excessive marking of the wood and prefer slag only.

Remember, more distress marks will show up after staining than will be noticed on the raw wood. Don't be misled by the number visible after a light rocking of the slag over the wood. There will be many. The stain will darken them and bring them out most vividly. The practice piece should be stained to show the actual effect.

3. STAINING

Most pieces shown in this book were stained with No. 314 walnut oil stain. See Section 6 for a supplier. This can be thinned with benzine or turpentine for those wishing a lighter color. Allow 8 to 10 hours to dry.

4. WASH COAT

Cover the stain with a thin wash coat of five parts alcohol to one part of four-pound-cut white shellac. Brush on quickly and lightly if it is impossible to spray. Allow 8 to 10 hours to dry. Sand *very* lightly with #320 silicon carbide paper.

5. SEALER COAT

This coat prepares the surface for the lacquer coats to come and is most important. A recommended lacquer sealer is Duco No. 1991. This can be thinned about 10% with Duco lacquer thinner No. 3656, which has a medium drying speed. Allow 2 hours to dry, then sand lightly with #320 silicon carbide paper. Proper drying is indicated by a white powder residue when sanded.

Important: If the piece is to be antiqued as in Step 6 (which is optional), it is necessary to thin out the sealer coat. Use half sealer and half lacquer thinner, and spray *very* lightly. Otherwise the glazing compound will not bond properly and can be wiped off the surface. Sand lightly with #320 silicon carbide paper.

6. ANTIQUING (GLAZING)

This optional step is important if it is desired to create an authentic aged effect to the piece. This effect will be predominent in the distress marks and in corners and crevices.

The glazing compound is made up of burnt umber ground in Japan and thinned with turpentine to the consistancy of cream. It is also possible to use burnt umber ground in oil and thinned with benzine to the same consistency. Be careful; if the compound turns dull looking and is difficult to wipe off, it was mixed too thick. If this should happen, simply remove it with a rag dampened in either turpentine or benzine and start over again. Do not allow the thick compound to set up before attempting to remove it, however.

Apply the compound liberally with a 1½" brush to about two to three square feet. Within two to three minutes rub with a soft cloth. The trick in this operation is to determine how much glaze is to be *removed* and how much is to be *rubbed* into the surface. The light and dark areas and the texture of the wood will determine this process.

In general, most of the compound will be rubbed off. However, it should be wiped liberally into all distress marks, corners and crevices. Next, remove most, *but not all*, of the compound from these areas with a soft cloth. Use a 1" brush (dry) to lightly brush over the areas mentioned above. This brings about an aged look to the piece. It takes light, fast brush strokes to create the desired effect. Do not "overbrush" or remove much compound. Allow to dry a half hour. No sanding is necessary.

Purchasers of this style of furniture often pay an extra charge to have this operation made to their custom specifications. Although it is not included as a routine step by all cabinet finishers, it is strongly recommended. It creates that quality effect which causes the completed piece to rise above the common place.

7. FIRST LACQUER COAT

If the piece has been antiqued as in Step 6, spray a *very light* coat of *thinned* lacquer over the glaze compound. A recommended lacquer is Duco No. 1655 Gloss, thinned half and half with Duco No. 3656 lacquer thinner.

If Step 6 was omitted, then spray a "wet" coat of lacquer, thinned about 20 per cent, over the sealer coat. While it can be sprayed full strength, this thinning is preferred.

8. SECOND LACQUER COAT

Each successive coat of lacquer can be sprayed on after 1 or 2 hours drying time. Each should also be thinned about 20 per cent. Sanding and rubbing are not usually needed between coats of lacquer.

9. THIRD LACQUER COAT

Same as Step 8. It is best to give surfaces receiving hard wear (pedestal table for example) 4 or 5 coats. Allow last coat to dry 10 or 12 hours before attempting to rub it down as explained in Step 10. This last coat must be thoroughly dry.

10. RUBBING COMPOUND

The final step is to rub the last coat of lacquer with a liquid, satin-finish compound such as No. 761. See Section 6 for a supplier. This is applied using #320 silicon carbide paper. Always rub with the grain of the wood. Even pressure applied to all surfaces is most important. Rub just enough to remove dust specks and slight irregularities. Be careful not to rub through the finish. It is possible to use 4/0 steel wool in areas such as the legs of the bellows coffee table or in corners where the abrasive might create minute scratches on cross grain.

After rubbing, polish all surfaces with clean cotton waste or a soft cloth to remove all traces of compound. This particular compound is excellent for producing the proper satin finish that creates a warm, rich appearance so desirable in this style of furniture.

ALTERNATE FINISHING SCHEDULE USING SHELLAC

1. *Give final sanding* using 6/0 garnet finishing paper. Distress and stain if desired.
2. *Apply* wash coat of five parts alcohol to one part shellac, dry 8 to 10 hours.
3. *Rub lightly* with 4/0 steel wool.
4. *Apply second coat* of four parts alcohol to one part shellac, dry 8-10 hours.
5. *Rub lightly* with 4/0 steel wool.
6. *Apply third coat* of four parts alcohol to one part shellac, dry 8 to 10 hours.
7. *Rub lightly* with 4/0 steel wool and apply paste wax, allow to dry and polish.

Note: Recommended shellac is a white shellac, four-pound cut (four pounds of lac resin to the gallon of alcohol). Three-pound cut would require less dilution. Drying time will vary with the weather.

SECTION 4

Hardware

HARDWARE to be selected for the furniture described in this book includes surface hinges, latches and porcelain knobs. These items can be readily purchased in most good hardware stores. The names of two major manufacturers of the hardware shown in the illustrations may be found in Section 6.

For those wishing to locate cast brass or wrought iron reproductions of authentic colonial hardware, the names of five manufacturers and dealers can be found at the beginning of Section 6.

Samples of the surface hinges found throughout the book are shown in Figure 2.

Porcelain knobs may be purchased with a hole in the center for front mounting, or solid for mounting from the back. This type knob also is made in a crackle finish for an aged effect.

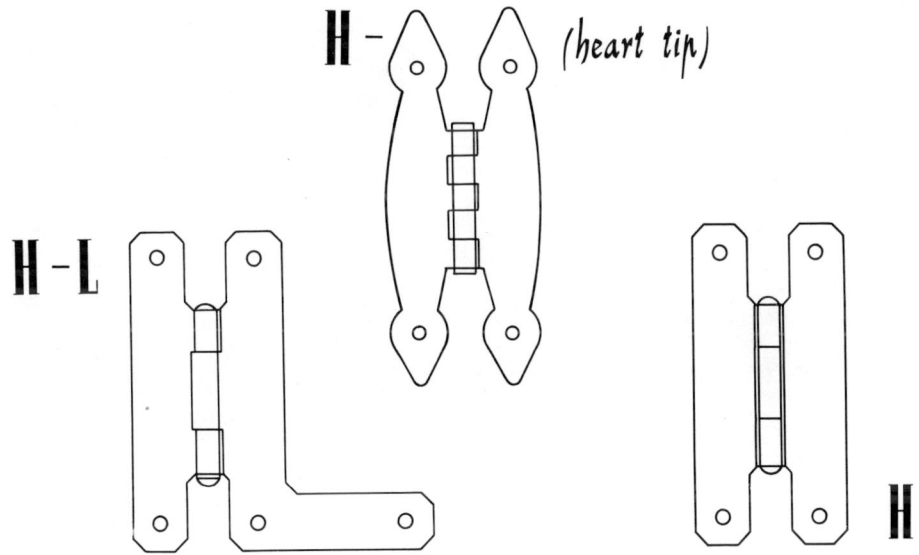

Fig. 2. Suitable Surface Hinges

SECTION 5

Construction Techniques

SEVEN DRAWINGS showing special techniques used in the construction of early American furniture are shown in this section. The techniques given in the plates are not the only ones possible but have been used successfully in quality cabinetmaking shops. They can be modified as needed.

Plate I illustrates some typical joints which allow wood to expand and contract to prevent shrinkage problems. *Plate II* shows four techniques of fastening tops on tables, cabinets, or benches. *Plate III* gives dimensions for two variations in the raised panel doors typical of colonial style cabinet work. *Plate IV* suggests details for constructing dovetailed drawers with a single center runner.

Plate V illustrates a possible method of roughly cutting the shape of ogee base molding on a circular saw, and also gives the set-up required to notch a turned pedestal to receive tripod legs. *Plate VI* suggests details for drop leaf hinges, dovetailed rails, kerfing to relieve warpage, joining top rails to legs, and screws which are countersunk and plugged. *Plate VII* illustrates some of the glue joints typical of this type of construction.

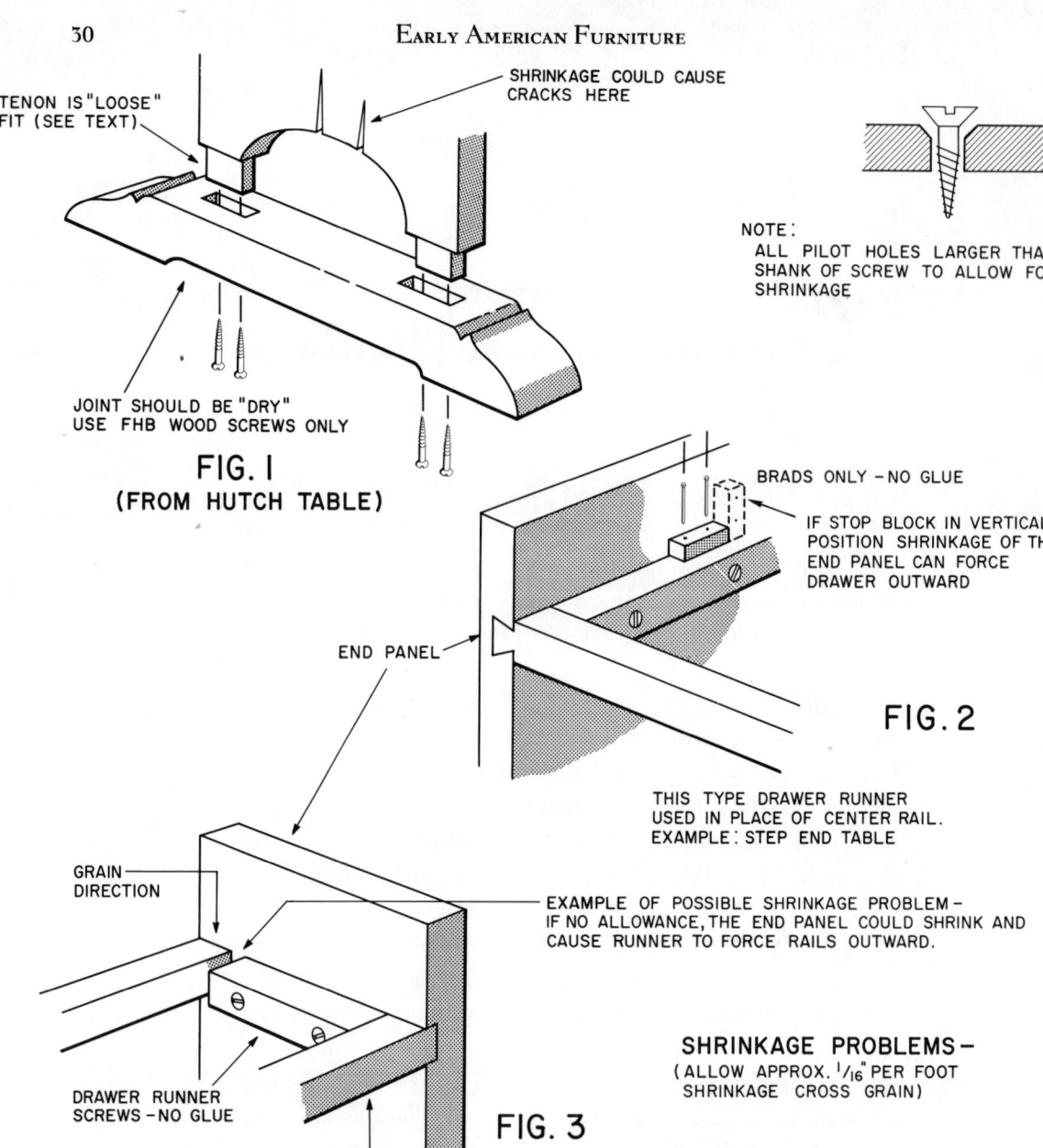

Fig. 1: A dry joint (no glue) is used to allow movement whenever a cross rail, runner, or cleat is fastened to a wide solid wood surface. This one requires two screws into each tenon. Mortise depth is less than half the thickness of the piece, see 17. Hutch Table.

Fig. 2: When the *stop block* is placed (with brads and no glue) on the runner, it cannot move forward. If placed on the end panel it could force the drawer forward when the end panel contracts. Thumb tacks may be placed in the drawer rails for smooth drawer movement.

Plate I. Shrinkage Problems

CONSTRUCTION TECHNIQUES 31

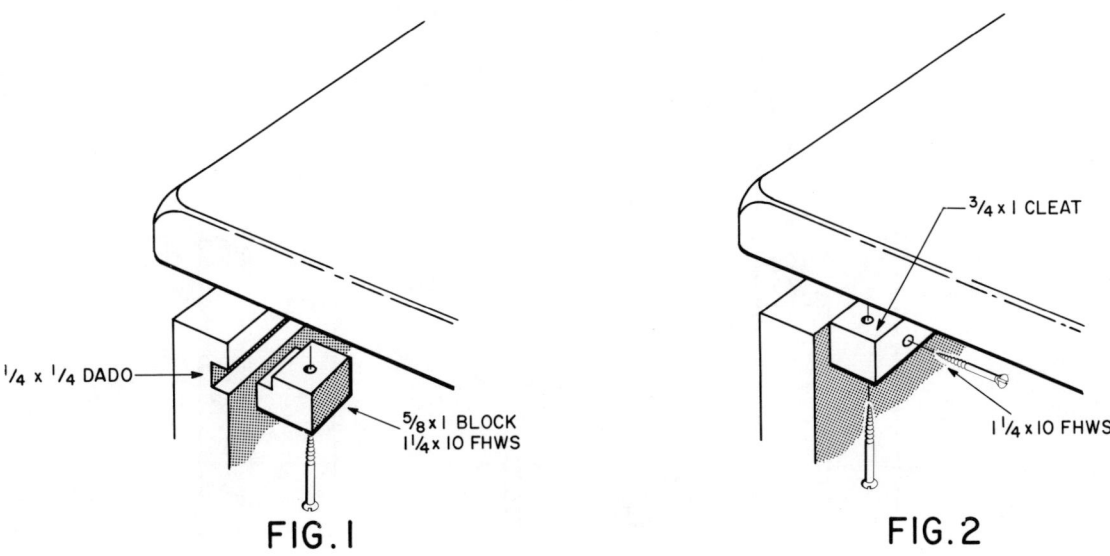

METHODS OF FASTENING TABLE TOPS

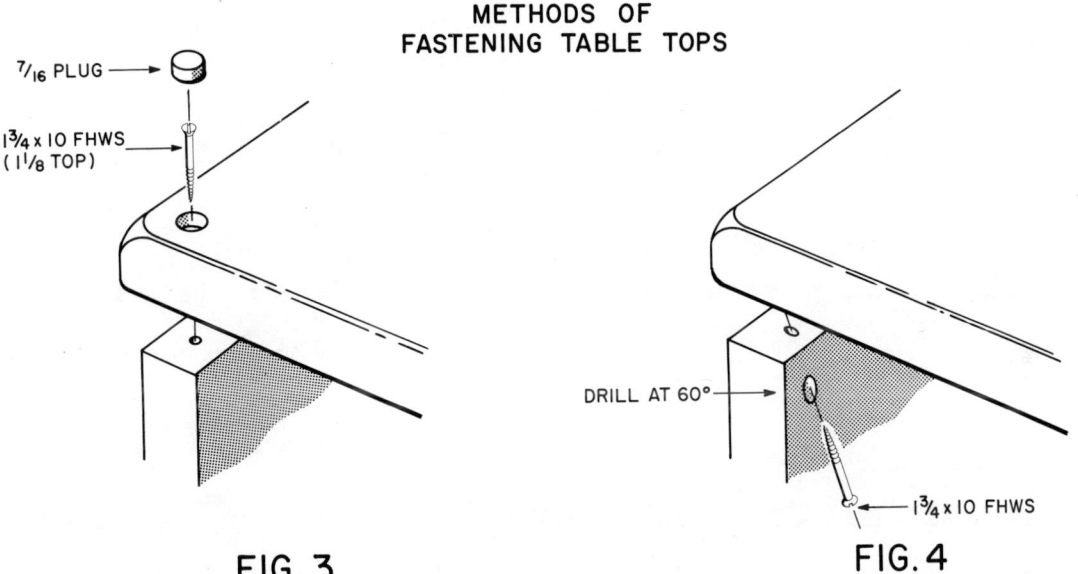

Fig. 1: This construction is commonly used when there is a top rail or skirt on all four sides. Blocks at front and back should not set all the way into the dado to allow the top to expand. The dado should stop short of the front if a through dado would be visible. *Fig. 2-4:* Shank hole for screws (except Fig. 1) must be elongated or enough oversize to allow tops to expand cross grain. The cleat fastener *(Fig. 2)* is shown on drawings for 11, 14, 15, 18, and 24. Plugged screws *(Fig. 3)* are used on pieces 12, 21, and 23. Slanted screws *(Fig. 4)* are shown on pieces 13, 16, and 20.

Plate II. Fastening Tops

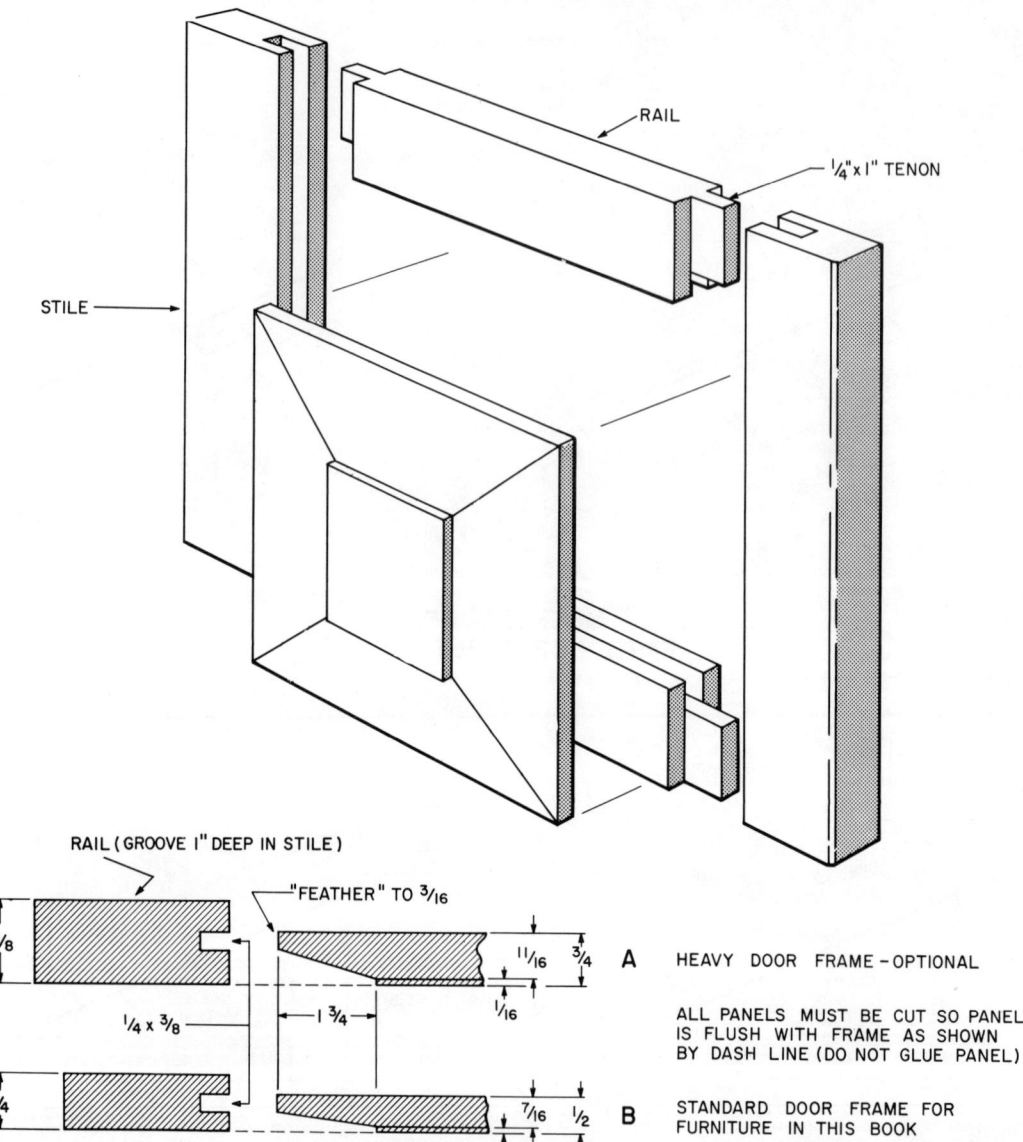

Two door frame thicknesses are shown. Style A is for a heavy effect preferred for larger pieces such as the hutch doors. Style B is the standard door because ¾" stock is more common and easily obtainable. Note the grove cut in the frame is deeper (1") in the stiles than in the rails (⅜"). Tenons should reach about halfway into the stiles for needed strength.

The raised panel may be cut on a circular saw (tilt the blade), or on a shaper using a cutter specially made for this purpose. The panel is not glued into the grooved joints so as to allow for expansion and contraction. When staining, apply stain liberally at the groove and panel joint so that it will not show raw wood if the panel should contract.

Plate III. Raised Panel Doors

Construction Techniques

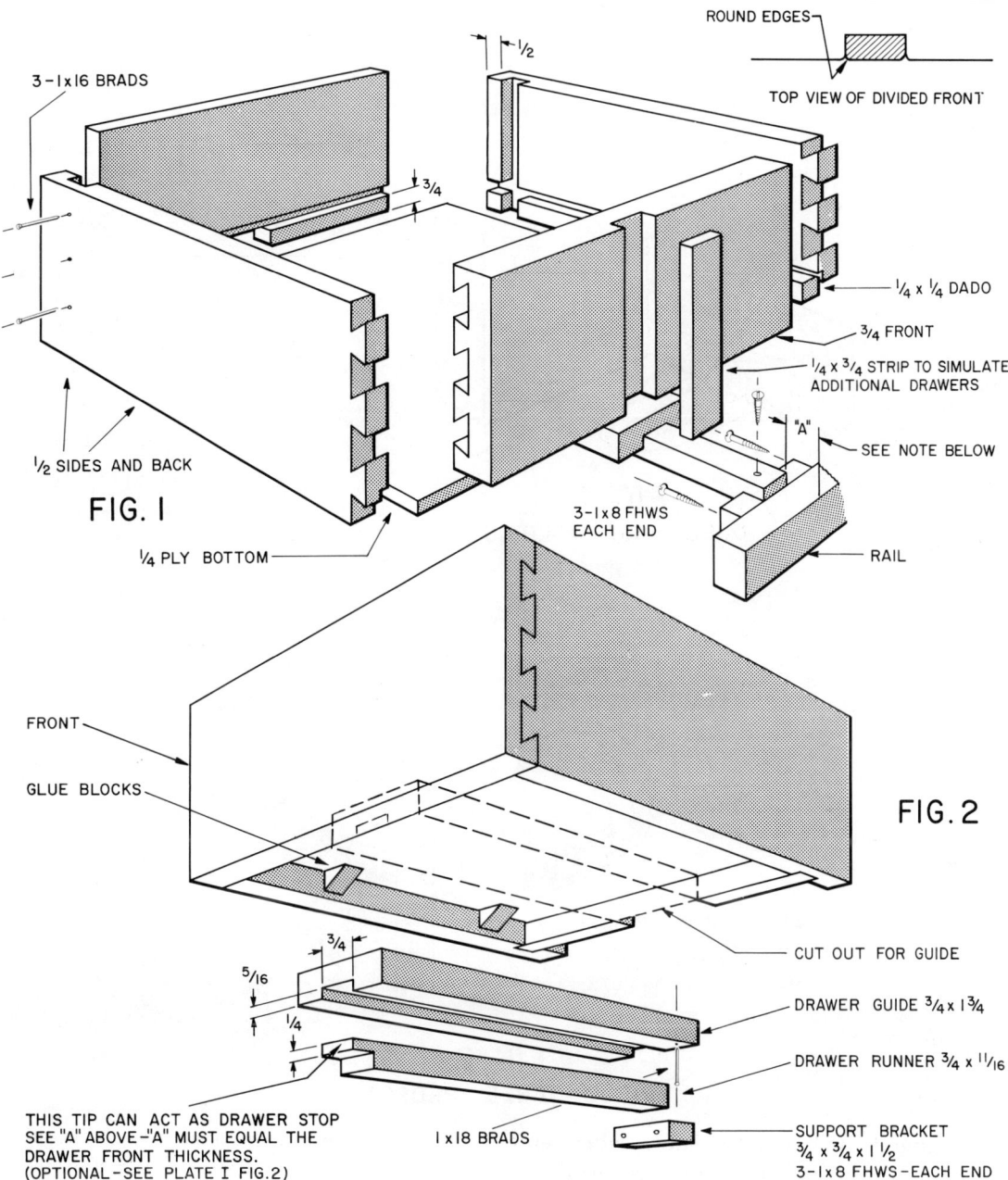

FIG. 1

FIG. 2

This is made using a dovetail attachment and a router-shaper. It can also be made with a simple rabbet cut—bradded and glued together. To simulate additional drawers (see 14) ¼" x ¾" strips may be glued into dado cuts of the same size in the drawer front. This reduces the work of making many smaller drawers and also gives the option of a larger drawer. Round all edges of the front and divider strips slightly.

Plate IV. Drawer Construction

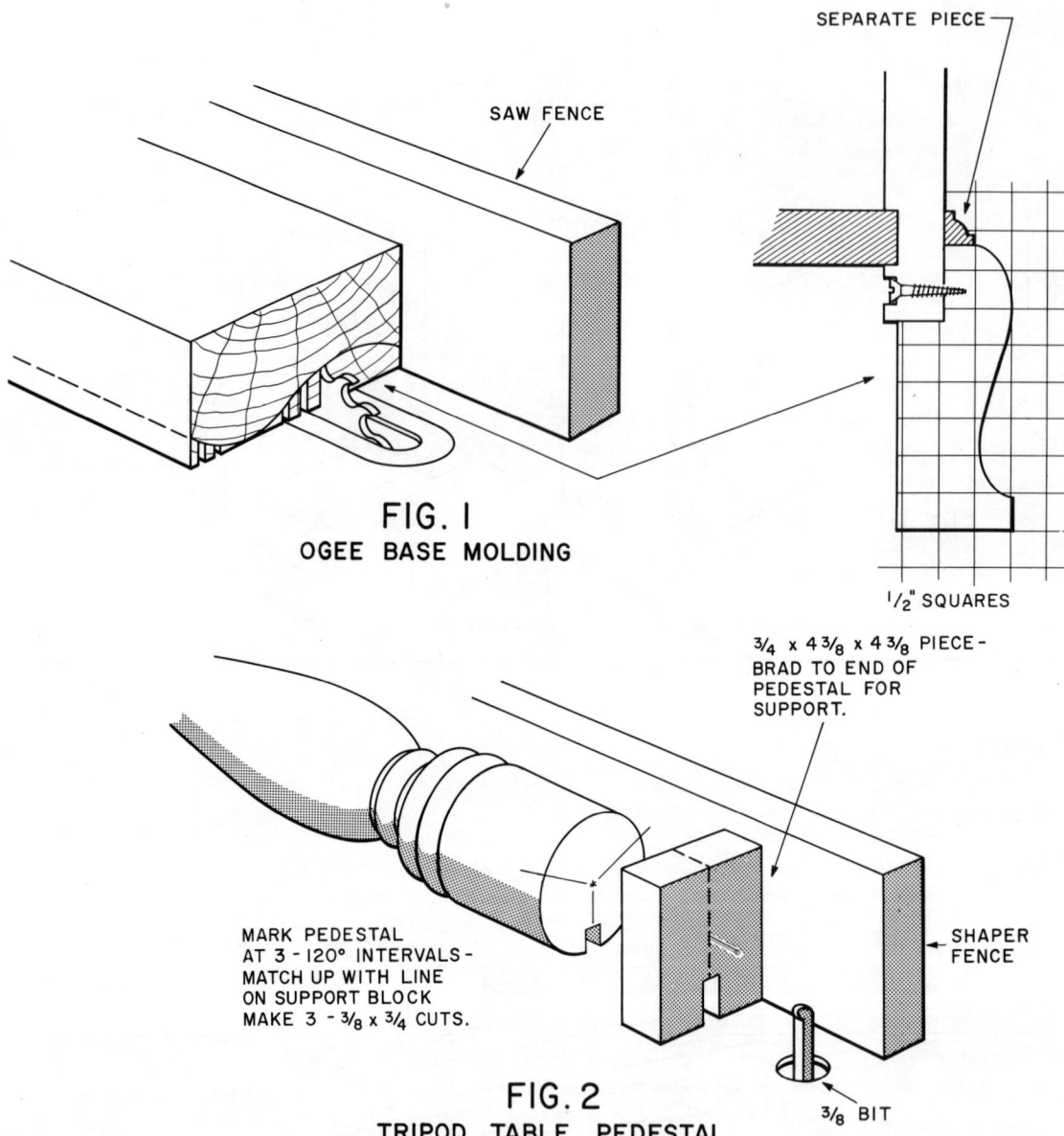

FIG. 1
OGEE BASE MOLDING

½" SQUARES

FIG. 2
TRIPOD TABLE PEDESTAL

Fig. 1: When large shaper cutters are not available for heavy ogee base molding, the circular saw can be used to make the basic cuts. The remaining shaping can be done with garnet paper. While plain uncurved bases are specified in the drawings, this style can be substituted.

Fig. 2: Be sure the brad shown is in the exact center of both the pedestal and the block. A second brad, off center and driven just enough to catch the pedestal, can be used to prevent it from shifting unexpectedly. It is easiest to align the guide marks at the top of the pieces.

Plate V. Special Cuts

Construction Techniques

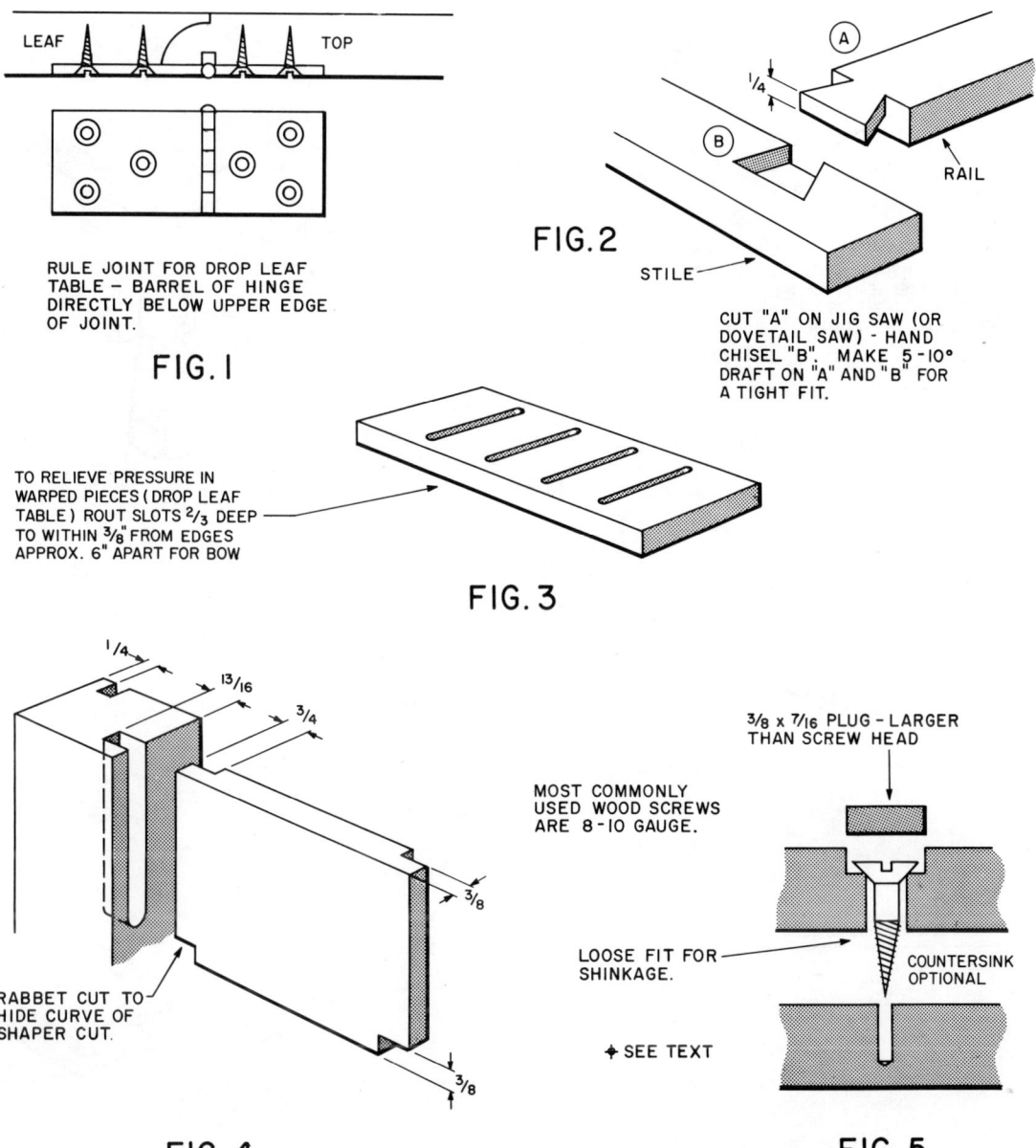

FIG. 1 — RULE JOINT FOR DROP LEAF TABLE — BARREL OF HINGE DIRECTLY BELOW UPPER EDGE OF JOINT.

FIG. 2 — CUT "A" ON JIG SAW (OR DOVETAIL SAW) - HAND CHISEL "B". MAKE 5-10° DRAFT ON "A" AND "B" FOR A TIGHT FIT.

FIG. 3 — TO RELIEVE PRESSURE IN WARPED PIECES (DROP LEAF TABLE) ROUT SLOTS 2/3 DEEP TO WITHIN 3/8" FROM EDGES APPROX. 6" APART FOR BOW.

FIG. 4 — RABBET CUT TO HIDE CURVE OF SHAPER CUT.

FIG. 5 — 3/8 x 7/16 PLUG - LARGER THAN SCREW HEAD. MOST COMMONLY USED WOOD SCREWS ARE 8-10 GAUGE. LOOSE FIT FOR SHINKAGE. COUNTERSINK OPTIONAL. ◆ SEE TEXT

Fig. 3: Grooving or kerfing the back side of a warped board may relieve tensions which cause the warpage. The kerfs should be crosswise to the warpage—about 1" apart in grain direction to relieve cupping or wind; about 6" apart cross grain to relieve bowing.

Fig. 5: The shank hole and the hole for the plug should always be larger than the screw to allow for expansion and contraction. Countersinking is optional as the screw will seat itself in soft wood such as pine. For ¾" stock use ¼" x ⅜" plugs.

Plate VI. Construction Details

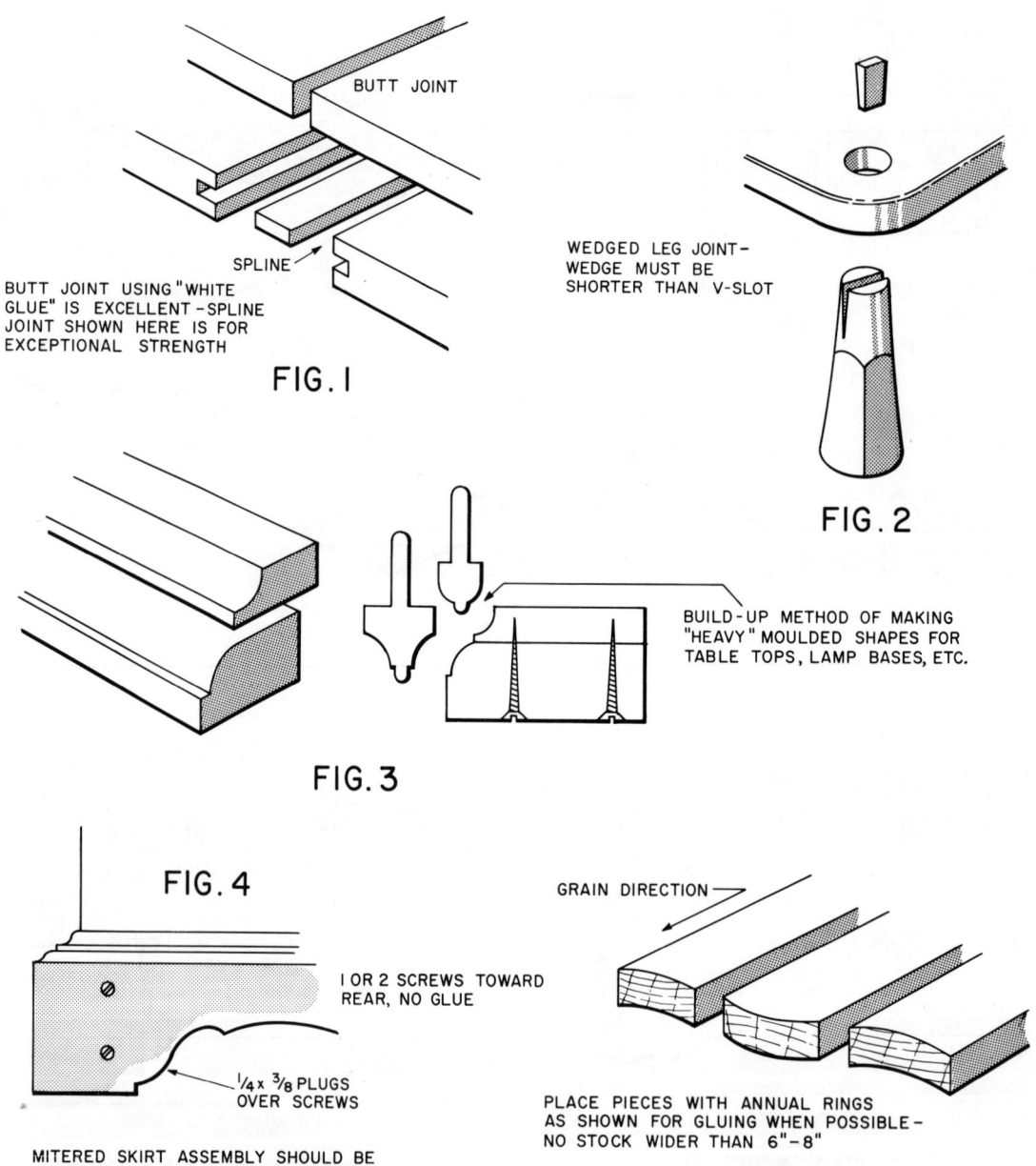

Fig. 1: Edge grain joints — splined and plain butt. The matched glue joint cut on a shaper is an excellent option. Splines are also valuable when one piece is plywood or end grain, but glue so as to allow possible end grain expansion and contraction.

Fig. 4: Use two wood screws and glue on the front skirt near the miter joint to hold the two pieces tightly together. At the back end of the side skirts use one screw but no glue to allow for expansion and contraction of the side panel.

Plate VII. *Gluing Problems*

SECTION 6

Suppliers

Although sources of supply will vary in different regions, several special ones are listed here. There are many more fine suppliers. Usually a local dealer can give the most assistance. Check with your local hardware dealers, lumber yards, or consult the product index of telephone directories.

REPRODUCTION HARDWARE:

Ball and Ball
  Whitford, Penna.

Don Streeter
  Iona, New Jersey

Period Furniture Hardware Co.
  123 Charles St.
  Boston 14, Mass.

18th Century Hardware Co.
  Ligonier, Penna.

Frank Horton
  Berlin, Conn.

EARLY AMERICAN STYLED HARDWARE:

  (Shown on various pieces in this book and obtainable at most good hardware stores).

McKinney Manufacturing Co.
  Pittsburgh 3, Penna.

Amerock Corporation
  Rockford, Ill.

FINISHING MATERIALS:

Industrial Finishing Products, Inc.
  465 Logan St.,
  Brooklyn 8, N.Y.

  (Manufacturers of #314 stain and #761 rubbing compound, see Section 3. Many other colors of colonial stain also available).

LAZY SUSAN HARDWARE:

  (Bearings)

Triangle Manufacturing Co.
  722 Division St.
  Oshkosh, Wis.

SECTION 7

Important Historical Collections of Early American Furniture

1. *Shelbourne Museum*
   7 miles south of Burlington, Vt.
   on U.S. Route #7
2. *Colonial Williamsburg*
   Williamsburg, Virginia
3. *Sturbridge Village*
   U.S. Route #20
   Sturbridge, Mass.
4. *Winterthur Museum*
   Winterthur, Delaware
   5 miles north of Wilmington
   on Route #52
   Reservations required
5. *Old Deerfield*
   Deerfield, Mass.
6. *Metropolitan Museum of Art*
   Fifth Avenue, at 82nd Street
   New York, N.Y.
   — American Wing.
7. *Greenfield Village*
   Dearborn, Michigan
   — Ford Collection
8. *Philadelphia Museum of Art*
   Parkway at Fairmont Avenue
9. *New York Historical Society*
   170 Central Park West
   New York, N.Y.
10. *The Art Institute*
    Michigan Avenue at Adams St.
    Chicago, Ill.
11. *Baltimore Museum of Art*
    North Howard St.
12. *Valentine Museum*
    Richmond, Virginia
13. *Detroit Institute of Art*
    5200 Woodward Avenue
14. *Wadsworth Atheneum*
    590 Main Street
    Hartford, Conn.
15. *Nelson Museum*
    Kansas City, Mo.
16. *San Francisco Art Museum*
    Van Ness Ave. at McAllister St.
17. *Museum of Fine Arts*
    465 Huntington Avenue
    Boston, Mass.
18. *Hunter House*
    Washington St.
    Newport, R.I.

Selected Pieces of Furniture

1. Foot Stool

THIS STOOL is a comparatively simple piece to construct and can be used in a practical manner various places in a den or living room. A popular setting is the front of a fireplace.

For those wishing to improve upon the stool, the addition of a red corduroy cushion with black buttons and black welting will add immensely to the appearance as well as comfort.

CONSTRUCTION NOTES

Of the pieces shown in the book, this is probably the least difficult to construct. It has few parts and is easily assembled. If possible, the stool should be made from 1⅛" stock to give a strong, rugged appearance.

Make certain the legs and brackets are firmly glued and screwed into position for necessary strength, The hand grip that is added to each of the ends should be filed and sanded to a half round shape and blended smoothly in the ends as well as the rear corners. The front edge of the seat should be thoroughly rounded over in the center area to indicate wear.

Bill of Materials

PART	QUANTITY	DESCRIPTION	DIMENSION
1	1	Back	1⅛ x 4½ x 24
2	1	Seat	1⅛ x 11¾ x 24
3	2	Ends	1⅛ x 4 x 12¾
4	2	End Grips	1⅛ x 1⅛ x 8½
5	2	Feet	1⅛ x 11 x 8
6	4	Foot Supports	1⅛ x 2½ x 4½
A	2	Flat Head Wood Screws	1¼ x 10
B	5	Flat Head Wood Screws	2 x 10
C	4	Flat Head Wood Screws	1¼ x 10
D	6	Flat Head Wood Screws	1¼ x 10
E	8	Flat Head Wood Screws	1½ x 10

Foot Stool

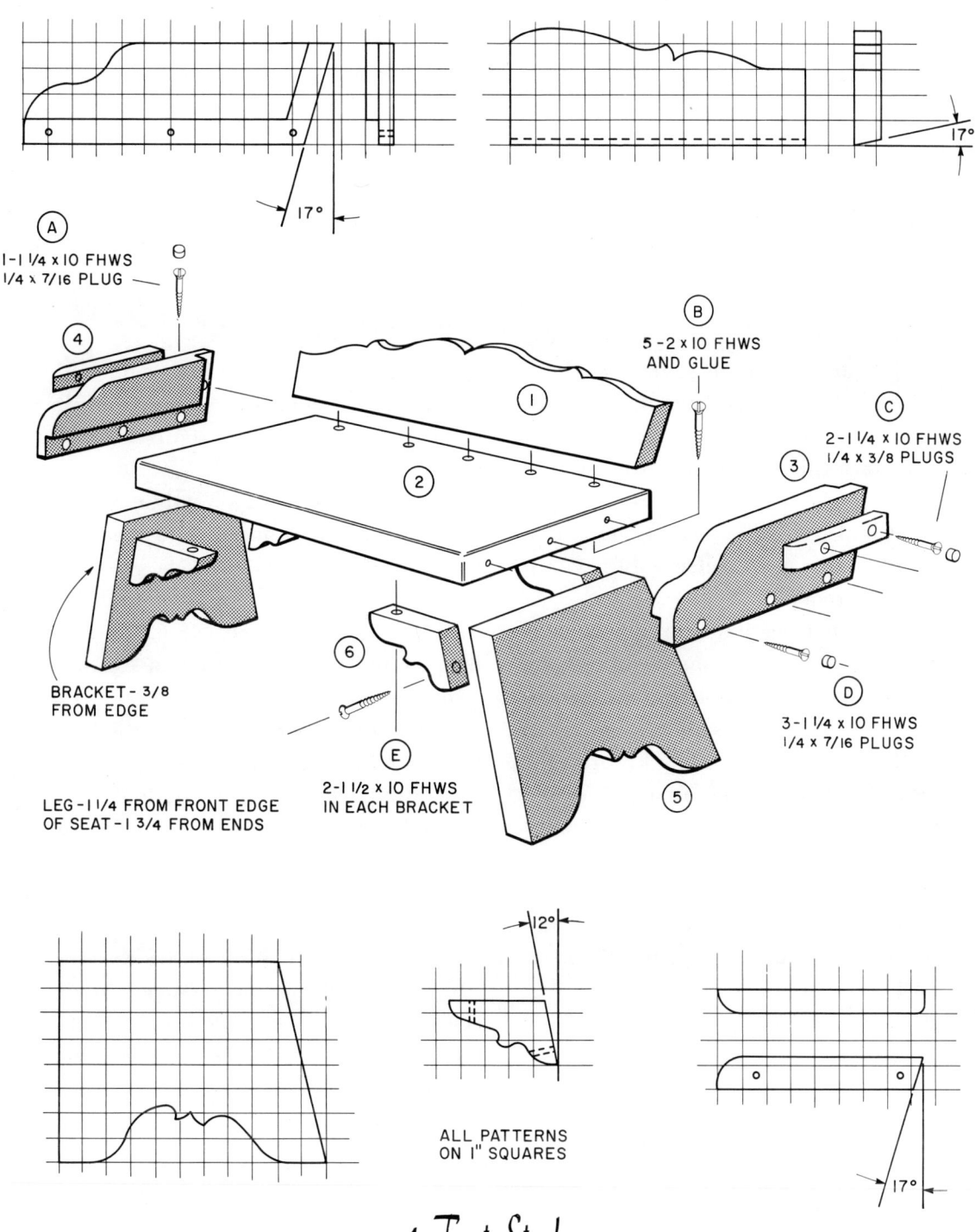

1. Foot Stool

2. Cranberry Picker Magazine Rack

HERE IS A UNIQUE PIECE that was (and still is in some areas) an important implement. The conversion of this cranberry picker to a magazine rack allows it to take over the important place next to a favorite reading chair. It also could become a companion piece to the gear coffee table within the same room.

Another possibility for this piece is to reduce the dimensions given here by approximately one half, and wire it for use as a lamp. Brass pipe is mounted at the center of the back, brought straight upward, and arched forward so as to center the light socket. The magazine section can be used to hold natural or synthetic plants. The reflection of light upon the green leaves with the proper light bulb and lamp shade is most effective.

CONSTRUCTION NOTES

This is one of the less difficult pieces of the collection to construct. It uses simple butt joint construction throughout.

The handle is thoroughly rounded with a file and sandpaper to create a worn look. The same look is given to the 3/8" dowel rods that should be heavily distressed. See Step 2 of the lacquer finishing procedure in Section 3 for this operation.

Cut the end pieces (1) by lightly bradding them together so as to produce exact duplicates when cutting to shape. Assemble the upper section including the bottom piece (2) as one unit. Fasten the feet and dowel rods into position last.

Front and rear panel widths are suggested and can be changed to fit stock on hand — the effect of a three piece panel should be retained for proper effect.

Cranberry Picker Magazine Rack

Bill of Materials

PART	QUANTITY	DESCRIPTION	DIMENSION
1	2	Ends	¾ x 5¾ x 18½
2	1	Bottom	¾ x 5¾ x 16
3	1	Lower Front	¾ x 1¾ x 16
4	1	Center Front	¾ x 4 x 16
5	1	Upper Front	¾ x 2¾ x 16
6	1	Lower Back	¾ x 4 x 14½
7	1	Center Back	¾ x 2¾ x 14½
8	1	Upper Back	¾ x 2¾ x 14½
9	2	Feet	1½ x 2 x 10½
10	1	Handle	¾ x 2½ x 14
11	14	Dowel Rods	⅜ x 9½
A	2	Flat Head Wood Screws	1½ x 10
B	4	Flat Head Wood Screws	1¼ x 10
C	30	Brads	1½ x 18

Cranberry Picker Magazine Rack

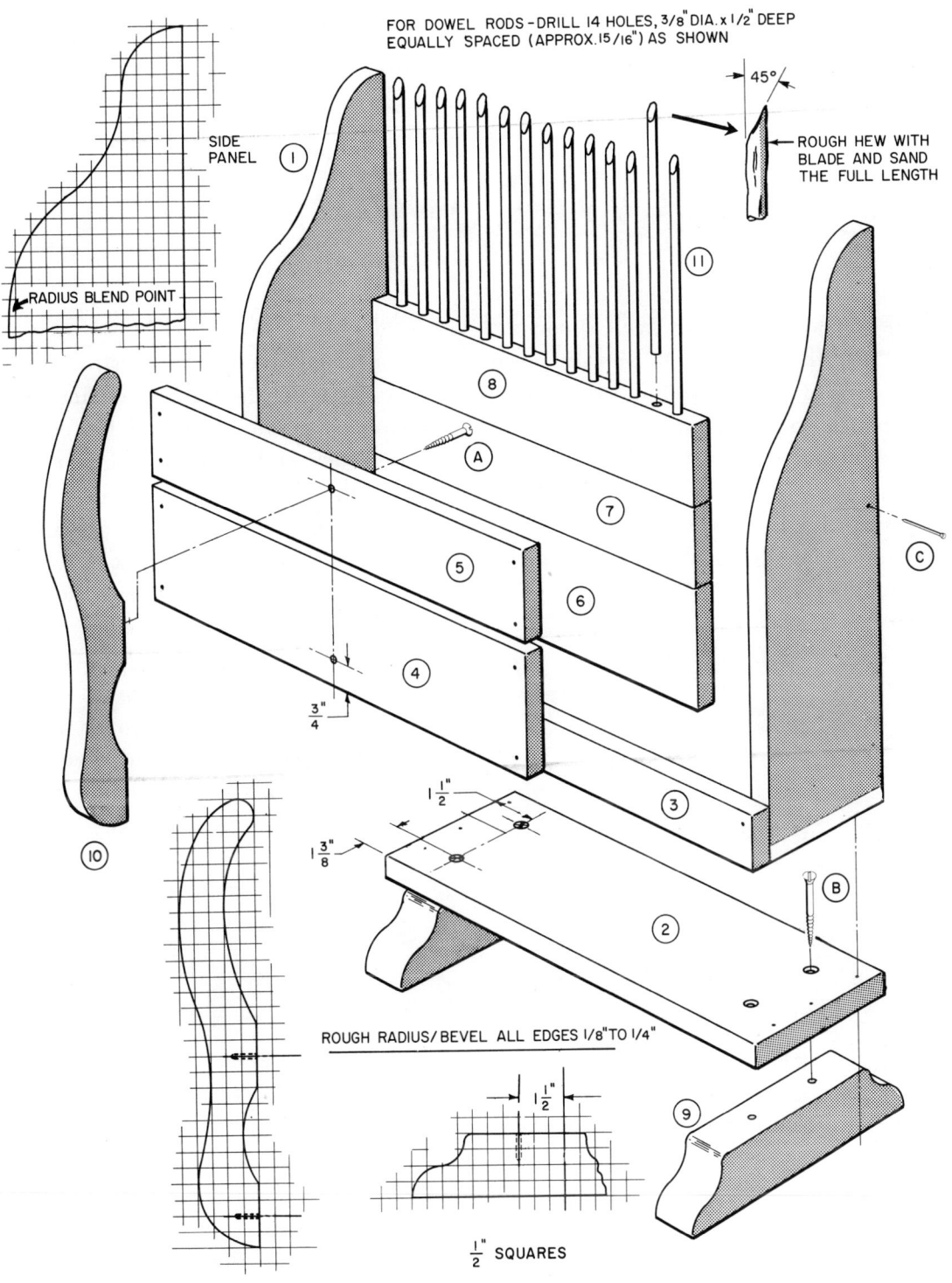

2. Cranberry Picker Magazine Rack

3. Wall Spoon Rack

Here is a sturdy wall spoon rack that adds depth and dimension to any wall and is attractive enough to grace many walls without additional accessories. The scroll design is typical of the Pennsylvania German Style. Drawers afford additional storage for silver and other small household items.

CONSTRUCTION NOTES

The main effort to construct this piece is that of the scroll back and the drawers. Thoroughly round the edges of the back and hand cut the star design with a small V-shaped hand carving tool (or similar tool) and sand the edges smooth. There is no hole in this design and the rack is fastened to the wall with standard wall fasteners.

Carefully cut and sand the spoon holders by checking with a typical spoon to be used in the rack for proper width of holder space. Brads and glue are sufficient for joints as there is little stress upon them.

Wall Spoon Rack

Bill of Materials

PART	QUANTITY	DESCRIPTION	DIMENSION
1	1	Upper Spoon Holder	½ x 1½ x 15½
2	1	Lower Spoon Holder	½ x 1½ x 13½
3	1	Back	½ x 20 x 31
4	2	Ends	¾ x 6 x 17½
5	1	Upper Shelf	¾ x 5½ x 14¼
6	1	Lower Shelf	¾ x 5½ x 14¼
7	1	Bottom	¾ x 6¾ x 16½
A	20	Brads	1¼ x 18
B	8	Brads	1 x 18
C	4	Wooden Knobs	¾ Dia.

Wall Spoon Rack

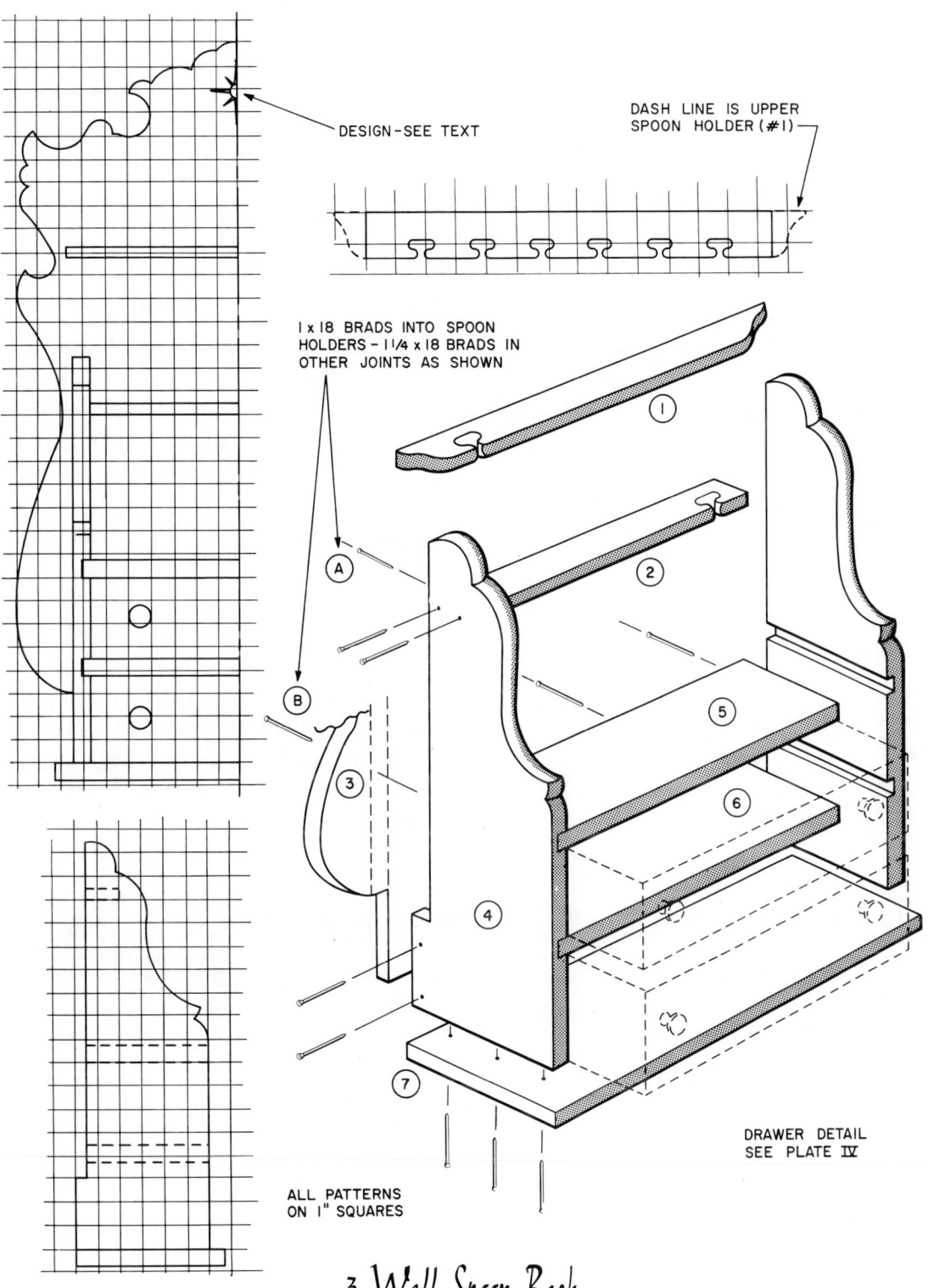

3. Wall Spoon Rack

4. Magazine Rack

THE SOMEWHAT RUGGED LOOK about this practical magazine rack makes it an interesting piece involving rather simple construction. This is the smaller of the two shown in this book. However, the center divider allows for ample storage of magazines. Splayed legs add to a well proportioned design and the height allows it to be placed near most furniture.

CONSTRUCTION NOTES

The basic construction of this piece is comparatively simple.

Layout and assemble the ends, front, center, back panels (and top rail) into one unit using brads and glue. Place this assembly on the base allowing for overhang as indicated on the drawing. Mark off light guide lines on the base and drill eight shank holes for the screws that will fasten the base to the upper section.

Cut the legs for a splayed angle outward in both directions, 10° each way. Drill and countersink five shank holes in each of the support blocks. Glue and screw the support blocks to each of the legs. Then glue and screw the support blocks to the base as indicated on the drawing.

Bill of Materials

PART	QUANTITY	DESCRIPTION	DIMENSION
1	2	Ends	3/4 x 8 1/2 x 13 3/4
2	4	Back Panels	1/2 x 5 1/16 x 10 7/8
3	1	Center Panel	1/2 x 9 3/4 x 20 1/4
4	1	Front Panel	1/2 x 5 1/2 x 20 1/4
5	1	Rear Top Rail	1/2 x 3 1/4 x 20 1/4
6	1	Base	3/4 x 9 1/2 x 22
7	4	Support Blocks	3/8 x 2 1/2 x 2 1/2
8	4	Legs	1 3/4 x 1 3/4 x 7
A	8	Brads	1 1/2 x 18
B	4	Flat Head Wood Screws	1 x 10
C	16	Flat Head Wood Screws	1 x 8
D	8	Flat Head Wood Screws	1 1/2 x 8

Magazine Rack

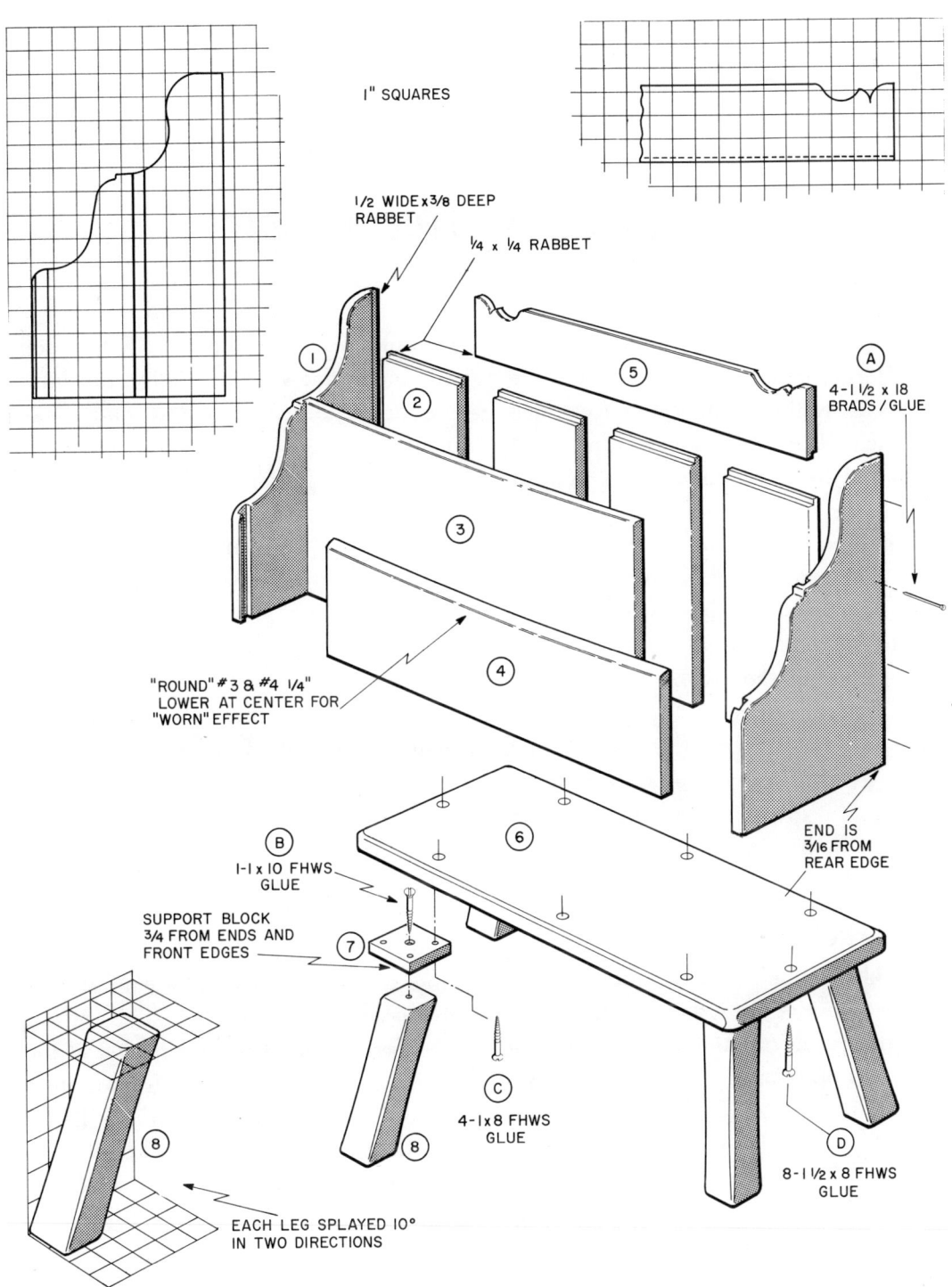

4. Magazine Rack

5. Gear Coffee Table

FOR THOSE who want something truly different in a coffee table, as well as something extremely practical, this style is most unique. It is bound to be as popular a conversation piece as it has been for the author in his own home. The gear is reminiscent of the old grist mills and saw mills. A *lazy susan bearing* allows the top to rotate smoothly on an old fashioned sugar bucket or *kanakin*.

The insertion of the *butterfly* is optional, but it adds the rugged look of the gearing devices found in old mills. The grain direction in the butterfly (across both wings) should be crosswise to the grain of the gear.

CONSTRUCTION NOTES

The kanakin can be purchased in stores dealing in early American accessories or in unpainted furniture. For proper proportion, try to obtain a kanakin about the size shown on the drawing. Slight variations would be permissible, but this is a popular size.

The gear is built up (butt glued) from three pieces of 3" (rough size) stock. If difficult to obtain, this size can be built up by laminating. Clamping becomes somewhat unwieldy, but laminating is quite possible and could make a strong top.

The gear should be heavily rasped, filed and sanded to round the sharp edges of the teeth on the underside of the gear but not as much as the upper side.

Note the 8° bevel on the butterfly and the reverse draft in its well to make a tight fit. Cut the 3/8" well with a router or chisel. While the butterfly could be cut from thinner stock, 3/4" is used because it is less apt to split. Apply glue and drive it in firmly with a mallet and a block of wood. Remove excess thickness with a plane or belt sander. Bore four 1" holes 3/8" deep, plug, and sand flush. The gear should be heavily distressed.

See Section 6 for a supplier of the bearing. Suggestions for its mounting should come with it. Rout the lid to fit the rim of the bucket. Press it in place with no glue so there is access to the bearing. The weight of the top is more than enough to keep it from tipping if it is bumped.

Gear Coffee Table

Bill of Materials

PART	QUANTITY	DESCRIPTION	DIMENSION
1	1	Butterfly	¾ x 10 x 12
2	4	Plugs	½ x 1 dia.
3	1	Top	3 x 30 x 30
4	1	Lid	¾ x 13 (Plywood)
5	1	Sugar Bucket	11 high, 13 base, 11 top
A	1	Lazy Susan Bearing	12 dia.

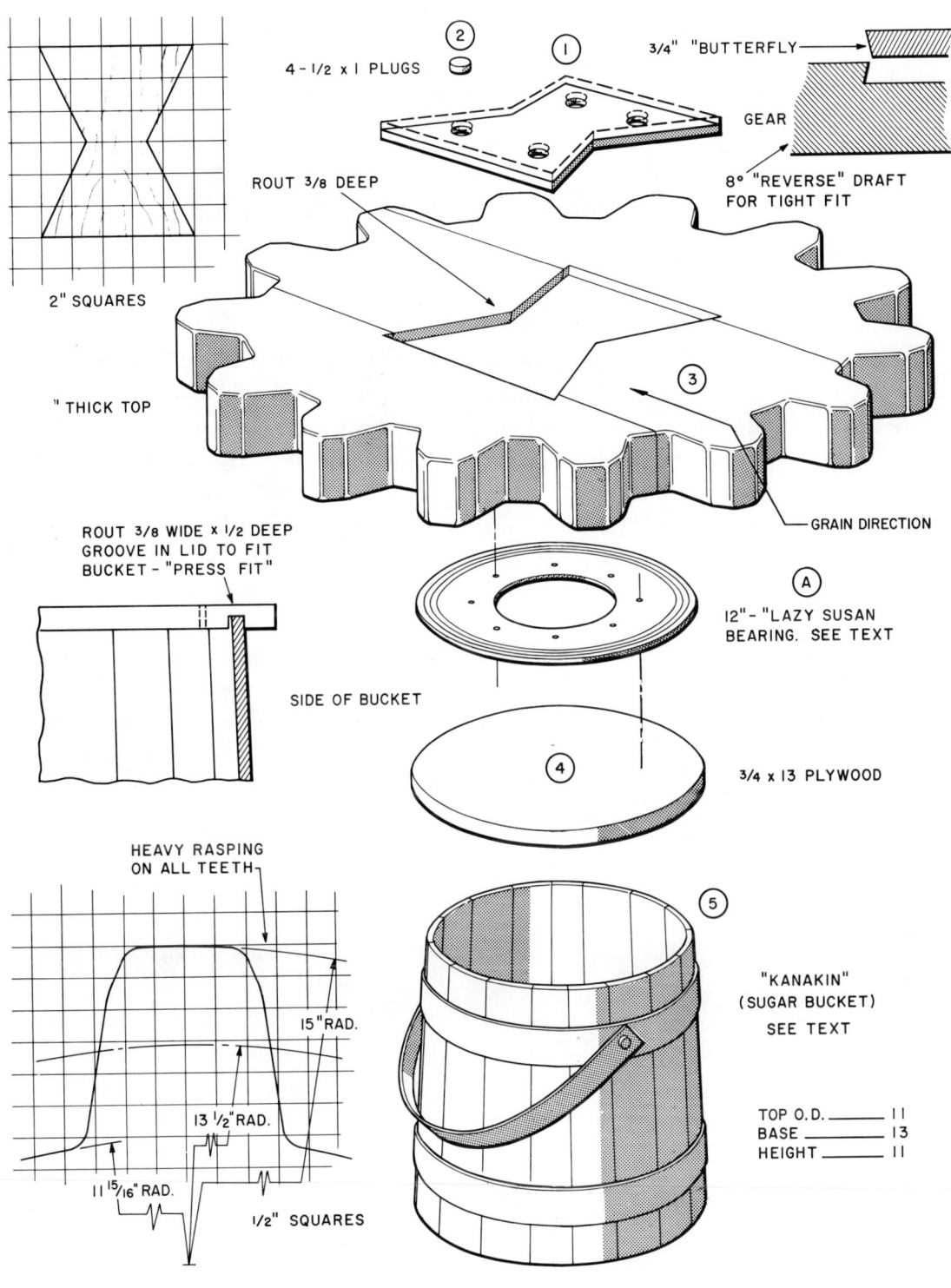

5. Gear Coffee Table

6. Bellows Coffee Table

ANOTHER UNUSUAL STYLE for a coffee table is this one inspired by the village blacksmith's bellows. The use of this table need not be limited to coffee service, but can be utilized as shown here in front of the fireplace. The rugged construction makes this piece withstand wear and tear from children as well as adults.

CONSTRUCTION NOTES

The top of the bellows can vary somewhat. It should not be less than 1¾" thick (1⅜" is too thin), but 2⅜" is desirable if it can be obtained. If necessary, a skirt could be built up from ¾" stock. Cut out the end hand hold before gluing top together.

Layout the legs, make 12° splay angle on the disk sander, band saw, or by hand. Attach blocks to the top of all three legs, locate and screw into position on underside of the top. Position rear stretcher on the rear legs, mark and cut as indicated. Drill six holes in rear stretcher, counterbore and fasten to the rear legs. This will now allow for accurate measuring and cutting of the center stretcher. Lengths listed allow for slight variations which might affect the two stretchers.

The nozzle specifications are for a 2⅜ top. If top is thinner, reduce the diameter of the nozzle proportionately.

Bellows Coffee Table

Bill of Materials

PART	QUANTITY	DESCRIPTION	DIMENSION
1	1	Cross Brace	1¾ x 3⅛ x 25
2	1	Top	2⅜ x 31 x 49½
3	1	Nozzle	2¾ x 2¾ x 7¾
4	3	Legs	2¾ x 2¾ x 15
5	1	Center Stretcher	1⅜ x 3 x 27
6	1	Rear Stretcher	1⅜ x 3 x 28
7	3	Leg Blocks	¾ x ¾ x 4
A	2	Flat Head Wood Screws	2½ x 10
B	2	Flat Head Wood Screws	3½ x 10
C	4	Flat Head Wood Screws	3½ x 12
D	15	Flat Head Wood Screws	1½ x 10
E	4	Flat Head Wood Screws	1¾ x 12

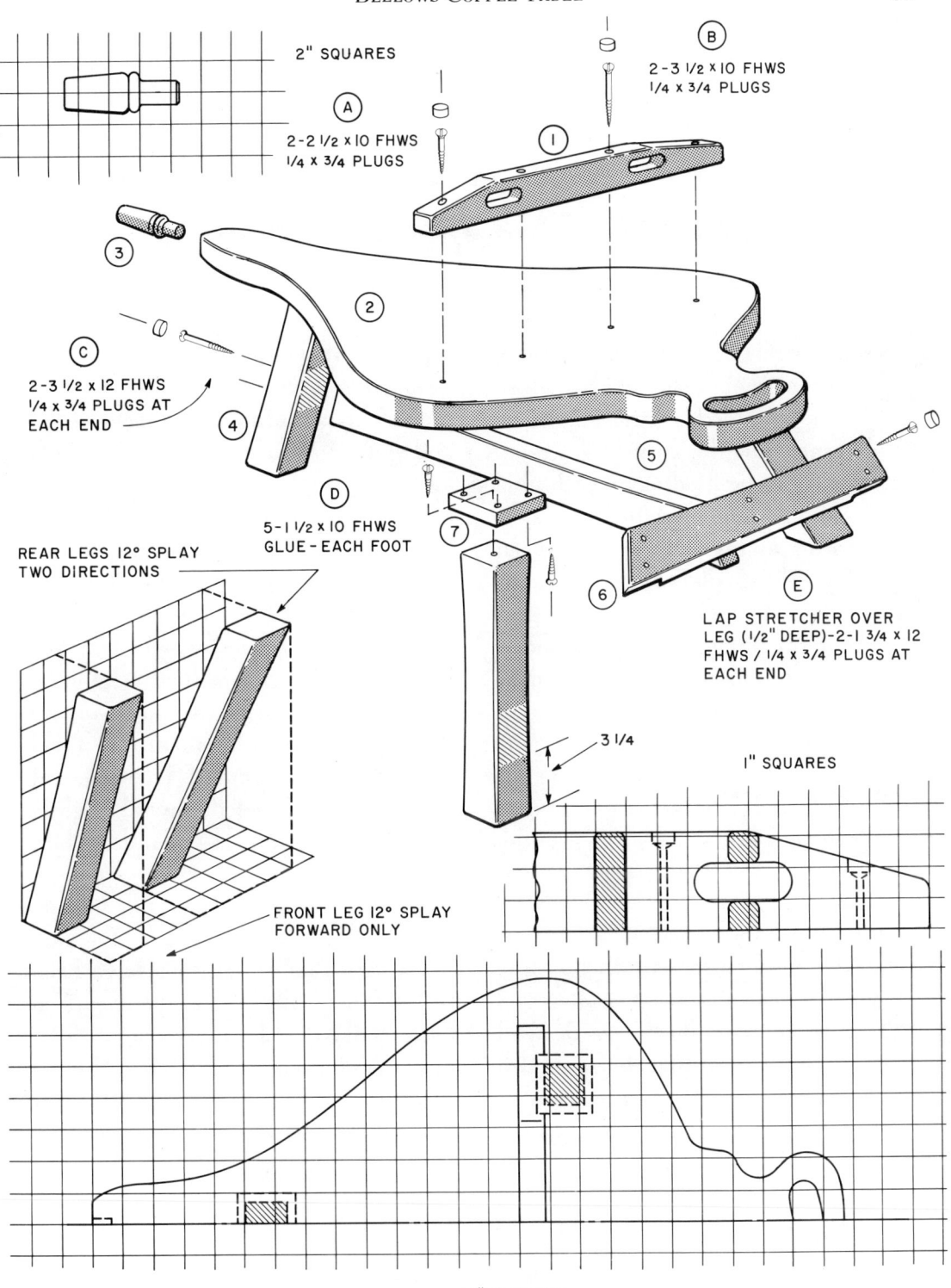

6. Bellows Coffee Table

7. Butter Churn Table

THE BUTTER CHURN is not only reminiscent of colonial living but has remained on the American rural scene until the very recent past. This piece can be used as an end table (legs can be shortened to fit sofa or couch arms as needed) or used as a table for a lamp placed in the corner of a room as shown here.

Butterfly hinges are recommended for the top. They have been placed near the back to allow for lamps that might have large bases.

CONSTRUCTION NOTES

Use care in assembling the crank shaft; it was purposely made with a long shaft. Curious hands are bound to turn the handle and with a short shaft the mechanism would be soon damaged. Note that the retaining pin (13) is placed close to the inside wall of end panel (4) so that the shaft can not be pulled out. All slats are nailed in place except for two or three at the bottom to allow for working space to assemble the shafting.

To make a full sized layout of the end view, draw a rectangle $11\frac{3}{8}''$ wide and $12\frac{3}{4}''$ high. Draw the bottom curvature with a radius of $5\frac{11}{16}''$. Then draw in the side panels and slats. It will be necessary to file a series of flats into the curvature of the end panels so each $1\frac{1}{2}''$ slat has a spot on which it fits. Locate upper pieces first, beginning with the side panels (5) and working downward. The bottom slats are fitted to the space remaining. The edges of each slat are beveled inward slightly for a snug fit around the rather short radius.

The churn should be rather heavily "distressed." Carefully strike the nail holes with slag (after nails have been set) to make them inconspicuous. The holes could also be covered with filler or with antiquing (see Step 6 in Section 3). Another option is to sink the nails about $\frac{1}{4}''$ and cover with $\frac{1}{4} \times \frac{7}{16}$ plugs.

Butter Churn Table

Bill of Materials

PART	QUANTITY	DESCRIPTION	DIMENSION
1	1	Stationary Top	3/4 x 3 1/2 x 15 1/2
2	1	Movable Top	3/4 x 10 7/8 x 15 1/2
3	1	Cleat For Top	1 x 2 x 8 1/2
4	2	End Panels	3/4 x 11 3/8 x 12 3/4
5	2	Side Panels	3/4 x 7 x 14
6	1	Bottom	3/4 x 11 3/8 x 12 1/2
7	12	Slats	3/4 x 1 1/2 x 14
8	4	Legs	1 3/8 x 2 1/4 x 25 1/2
9	2	"A" Frame Stretchers	1 3/8 x 2 1/4 x 14 1/4
10	1	Center Stretcher	1 3/8 x 2 1/4 x 14
11	1	Collar	1 1/2 x 2 3/8 dia.
12	1	Shaft	1 dia. x 16 7/8
13	1	Retaining Pin	3/8 dia. x 1 1/4
14	1	Crank Pin	3/8 dia. x 2
15	1	Crank Arm	1 3/8 x 3 1/4 x 7 1/4
16	1	Crank Handle	1 1/4 x 1 1/4 x 3 3/4
A	1 pair	Butterfly Hinges	1 3/4 x 2
B	3	Flat Head Wood Screws	1 1/2 x 12
C	48	Finishing Nails	1 1/2 (4d)
D	8	Flat Head Wood Screws	1 3/4 x 12
E	8	Flat Head Wood Screws	3 x 10
F	4	Flat Head Wood Screws	2 x 10

Butter Churn Table

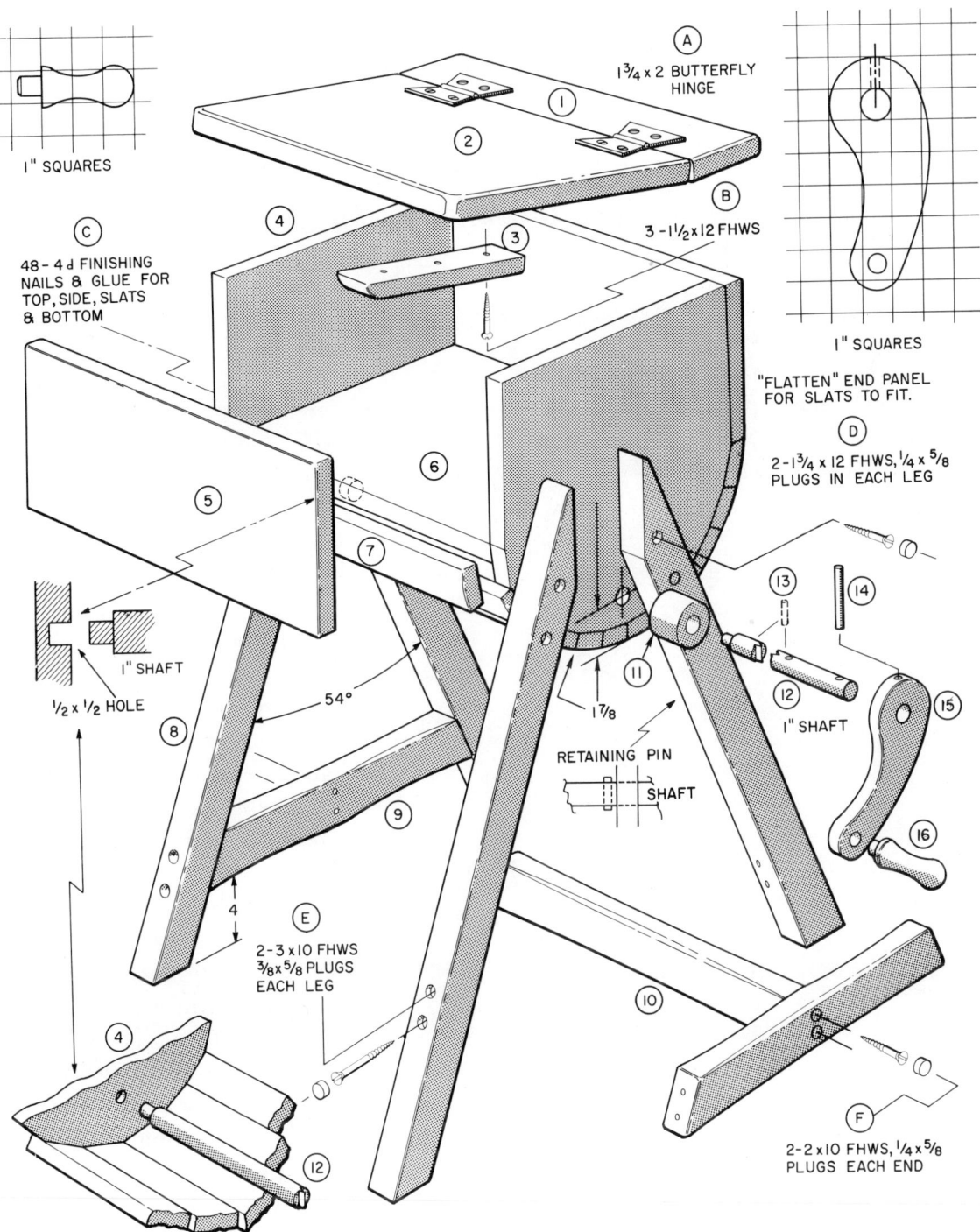

7. Butter Churn Table

8. Pedestal Table

A FINE ADDITION to the dining room or den is this attractive, sturdy pedestal table. It allows comfortable seating of four or five people, and the circular top saves room space. Placement of the table may be in a corner, in the center of the room or in a bay window area to add depth.

CONSTRUCTION NOTES

The construction of this piece involves only five parts. Stock for the pedestal may be built up if necessary but care should be taken to match the grain as closely as possible.

The top requires care in the proper layout for gluing. The pieces making up the top should not exceed 8" in width; carefully match the grain and alternate the annual rings.

The cleat is applied to the underside of the top to prevent possible wraping. Make shank holes in the cleat about $3/32"$ larger than the screw gauge to allow for expansion and contraction. Use no glue on this joint.

Two #12 screws hold the half lap joint of the feet. After these are in place, drill shank and pilot holes for the two $5/16"$ x 6" lag screws which hold the leg assembly to the pedestal. The pilot hole for the lag screw threads should be only about half the root diameter of the threads. End grain holding power, especially in soft pine, is limited, so be careful when tightening these screws.

Pedestal Table

Bill of Materials

PART	QUANTITY	DESCRIPTION	DIMENSION
1	1	Top	$1\frac{3}{8}$ x 38
2	1	Cleat	$1\frac{3}{8}$ x 5 x 35
3	1	Pedestal	5 x 5 x $23\frac{5}{8}$
4	1	Foot	3 x 4 x 26
5	1	Foot	3 x 4 x 26
A	4	Flat Head Wood Screws	$2\frac{1}{2}$ x 14
B	12	Flat Head Wood Screws	$2\frac{1}{4}$ x 12
C	2	Flat Head Wood Screws	2 x 12
D	2	Lag Screws	$\frac{5}{16}$ x 6

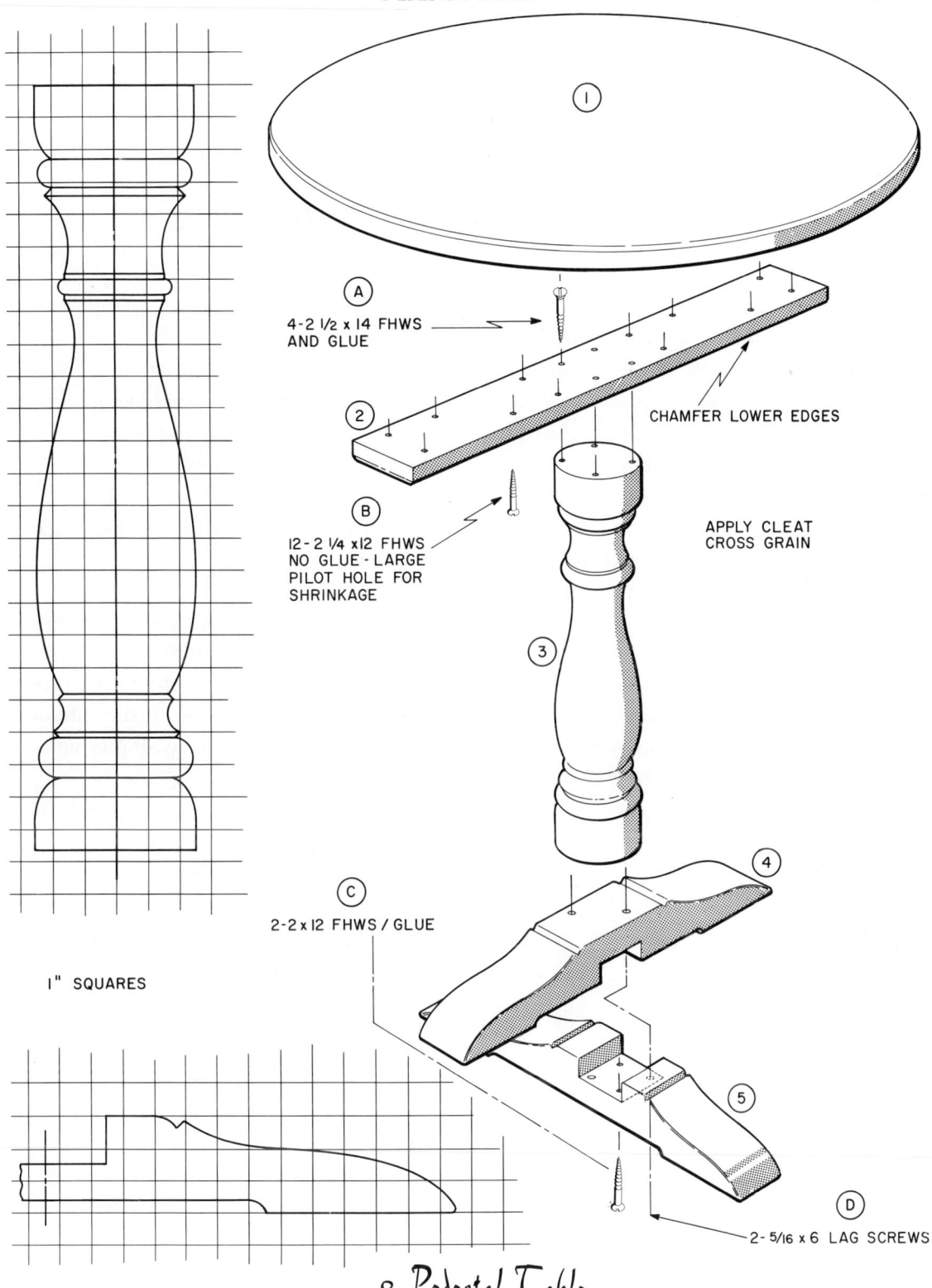

8. Pedestal Table

9. Apothecary Chest

This is a most interesting piece that lends itself to various uses. While called an apothecary chest, it could assume numerous roles in the home today. The drawers are not deep, but they offer ample storage space for small articles. The dimensions may be readily altered for larger storage space if desired. Such chests were originally quite shallow to store small packages of drugs.

The chest shown in the photo was made by the author to be used as a radiator cover. The heat was turned off in this case, thus avoiding louvered vents that would be needed for an "active" radiator.

CONSTRUCTION NOTES

The general construction of this piece is not particularly difficult. The most care probably is required in accurately cutting, assembling, and hanging the raised panel door. See Plate III for a complete drawing of door construction.

The molded base can be made in one piece which eliminates fitting separate molding to a square base. The shape of this molding is suggested and can be easily modified to fit the bits or cutters on hand, or the available commercial molding.

The front base (12) should be glued and screwed in position but the end base pieces (11) should be screwed with glue on miter only, using an oversize shank hole to allow for expansion or contraction that might pull the miter joint open. A small shoulder bead (not shown) may be cut in the top (1).

Apothecary Chest

Bill of Materials

PART	QUANTITY	DESCRIPTION	DIMENSION
1	1	Top	1⅛ x 9 x 27
2	2	End Skirts	½ x 2¼ x 5
3	1	Rear Skirt	½ x 2¼ x 25
4	2	Ends	¾ x 7½ x 23½
5	1	Upper Rail	¾ x 1¾ x 24¾
6	2	Cleats	¾ x 1 x 5¼
7	2	Partitions	¾ x 7⅛ x 8
8	2	Vertical Partitions	¾ x 7⅛ x 9½
9	3	Partitions	¾ x 7⅛ x 24¾
10	1	Back Panel	¼ x 23½ x 24¾
11	2	End Bases	¾ x 4½ x 8½
12	1	Front Base	¾ x 4½ x 27½
13	1	Front Base Support	¾ x 1 x 5
14	1	Upper Door Rail	¾ x 1⅝ x 6¼
15	2	Door Stiles	¾ x 1⅝ x 8¾
16	1	Lower Door Rail	¾ x 1¾ x 6¼
17	1	Raised Door Panel	¾ x 5¼ x 5⅞
A	10	Brads	1¾ x 18
B	12	Brads	1 x 18
C	3	Flat Head Wood Screws	1¼ x 8
D	2	Flat Head Wood Screws	1¼ x 8
E	5	Flat Head Wood Screws	1½ x 8
F	9	Porcelain Knobs	1"
G	1	Friction Latch	Small
H	1 Pair	Antiqued Butt Hinges	1⅜ x 2

Apothecary Chest

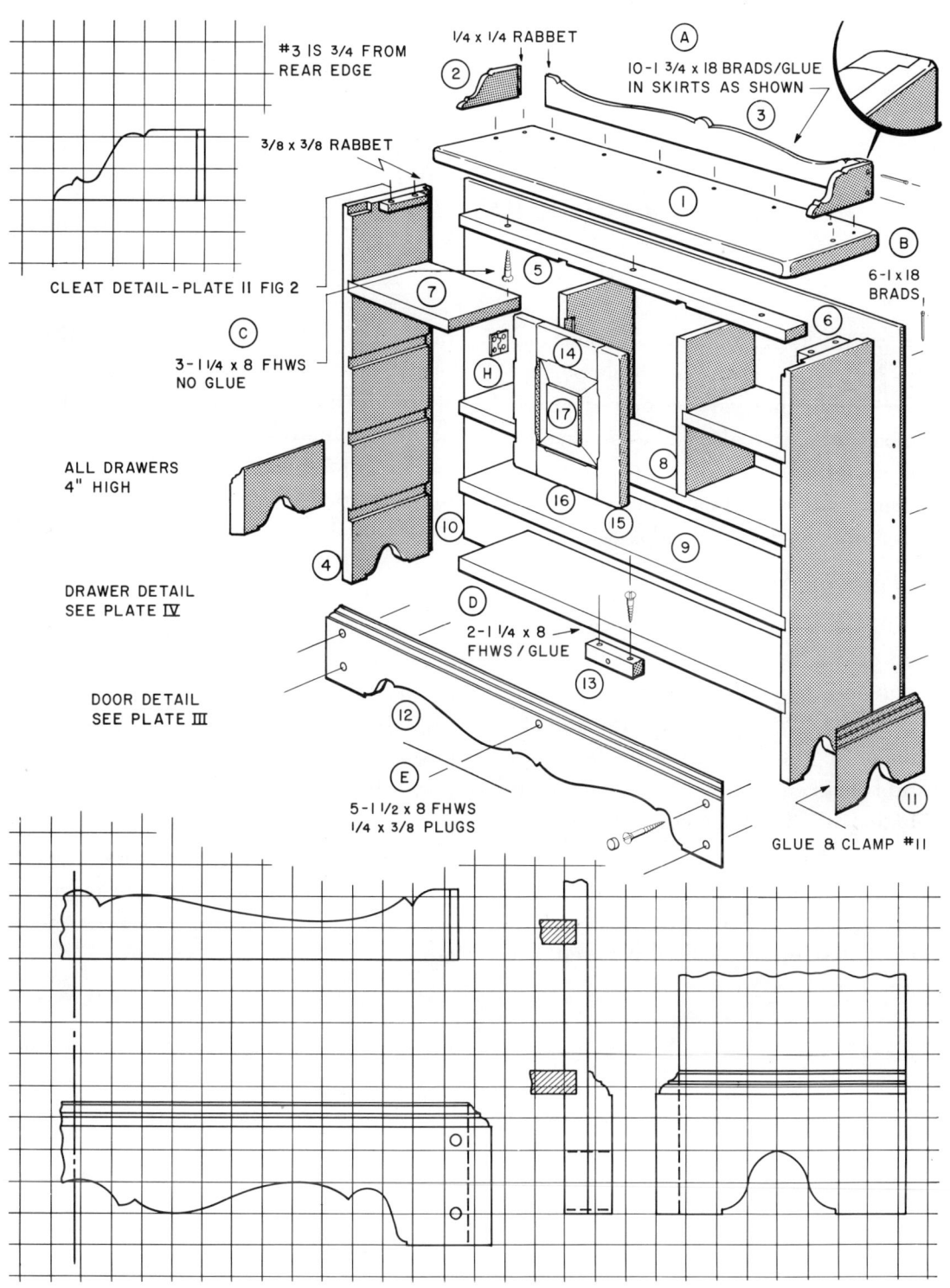

9. Apothecary Chest

10. Telephone Night Table

THIS TABLE may have various uses. It is shown as a telephone night table that can be placed next to a bed or chair. It also makes an excellent lamp table for reading purposes, with ample room for book storage as well as a drawer for odds and ends.

CONSTRUCTION NOTES

Construction of this piece is made up of two main units: the cabinet section and the pedestal section.

The two side pieces are rabbeted for a ¼" back panel with ⅜" x ⅜" rabbets in each side. Fasten the top and bottom to the sides using brads. The center shelf can be held in place with a minimum amount of glue only. The upper skirt is held with brads at the front part of the end pieces and with brads driven upward under the top piece along the back edge. Use glue sparingly here to avoid "squeeze out" around the narrow ½" stock.

The joint most critical for strength holds the pedestal (10) to the base (8). Take care that the pedestal wood screws (C and F) are fastened into rather small anchor holes (end grain holding power is less than cross grain). Screws may be dipped in glue. Allow glue to be absorbed into the end grain and to become tacky before joining the two pieces. If the 4" length wood screw is unavailable then ¼" x 4" lag screws may be used.

The two feet are half lapped and joined (before fastening to the pedestal) with 2" x #12 wood screws (H) and glue.

Telephone Night Table

Bill of Materials

PART	QUANTITY	DESCRIPTION	DIMENSION
1	2	Sides	¾ x 11 x 15
2	2	Upper End Skirts	½ x 2¼ x 6⅜
3	1	Upper Rear Skirt	½ x 2¼ x 12½
4	1	Top	¾ x 10⅝ x 13¾
5	1	Lower Top Skirt	½ x ⅞ x 11¼
6	1	Center Shelf	¾ x 10⅝ x 12
7	1	Bottom	½ x 10⅝ x 12
8	1	Base	¾ x 11½ x 13¾
9	1	Back Panel	¼ x 12 x 15
10	1	Pedestal	3¼ x 3¼ x 11½
11	1	Foot	3¼ x 2¾ x 12¾
12	1	Foot	3¼ x 2¾ x 12¾
A	10	Brads	¾ x 18
B	16	Brads	1½ x 18
C	3	Flat Head Wood Screws	2 x 12
D	8	Brads	1¼ x 18
E	4	Flat Head Wood Screws	1¼ x 10
F	2	Flat Head Wood Screws	4 x 14
G	1	Porcelain Knob	¾ dia.
H	2	Flat Head Wood Screws	2 x 12

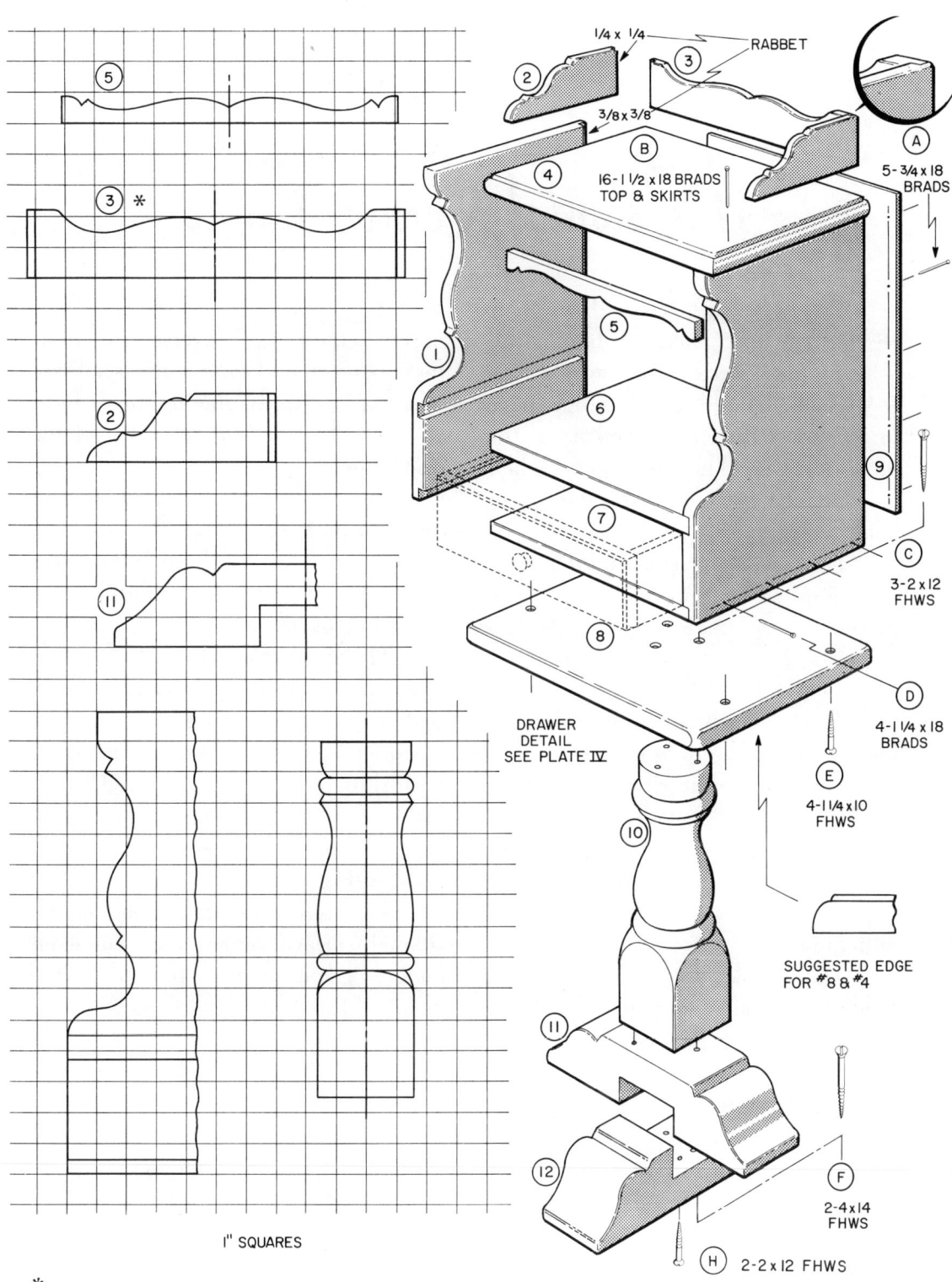

10. Telephone Night Table

11. Colonial Corner Table

THIS TABLE makes a fine multi-purpose piece for the corner of a room. It has practical storage space in the lower section as well as in the upper drawer. The open lower shelf area is excellent for book storage or knick-knacks.

The top is large enough for a reading lamp so that the table may be placed next to a chair.

CONSTRUCTION NOTES

The top construction uses cleats to hold it down. The front frame is shown with butt joints, although dovetail joints may be used, see Plate VI, Fig. 2.

Fasten the lower shelf (20) with screws as shown *before* inserting the enclosed bottom (12) which is held with glue only.

The shank holes for the screws holding the skirts in place should be approximately $3/32''$ oversize to allow for expansion and contraction, see Plate VII, Fig. 4. Apply glue to only a four- or five-inch area near the miter of the front skirt.

Base parts 16, 17 and 18 are fastened with brads and glue. To hide the brads (F) driven through the lower shelf (20), distress them carefully after they have been set.

The base trim (13, 14, 15) can be made from one piece and molded with a typical shoulder and ogee cutter. If cutter is not available, a separate molding may be purchased, and fastened with small brads and a minimum of glue. When purchasing, match the molding to the skirt.

The hardware shown includes H-shaped surface hinges and porcelain knobs. A friction latch is used on the inside of the door.

Colonial Corner Table

Bill of Materials

PART	QUANTITY	DESCRIPTION	DIMENSION
1	1	Top	$3/4$ x 15 x $29 1/2$
2	1	Side Panel	$3/4$ x $12 3/4$ x 22
3	1	Back Panel	$1/4$ x 22 x $27 1/8$
4	1	Side Panel	$3/4$ x $12 3/8$ x 22
5	2	Cleats	$3/4$ x $1 1/4$ x 12
6	1	Drawer Runner	$3/4$ x $1 11/16$ x $12 7/16$
7	2	Runner Supports	$3/4$ x $3/4$ x $1 1/2$
8	2	Frame Stiles	$3/4$ x $1 1/2$ x 22
9	1	Upper Rail	$3/4$ x 1 x 10
10	1	Center Rail	$3/4$ x 2 x 10
11	1	Lower Rail	$3/4$ x $3 1/4$ x 10
12	1	Bottom	$3/4$ x $13 5/16$ x 12
13	1	Side Base	$3/4$ x 3 x $14 3/8$
14	1	Front Base	$3/4$ x 3 x $14 3/4$
15	1	Side Base	$3/4$ x 3 x $1 3/4$
16	1	Shelf Base	$3/4$ x 3 x $4 1/8$
17	1	Shelf Base	$3/4$ x 3 x $12 3/4$
18	1	Shelf Base	$3/4$ x 3 x $4 5/8$
19	1	Corner Stile	$3/4$ x $2 5/8$ x 22
20	1	Lower Shelf	$3/4$ x $12 3/4$ x $15 1/2$
21	2	Door Stiles	$3/4$ x $2 1/8$ x $12 1/2$
22	1	Upper Door Rail	$3/4$ x $2 1/8$ x $7 1/4$
23	1	Lower Door Rail	$3/4$ x $2 3/8$ x $7 1/4$
24	1	Door Panel	$1/2$ x $6 3/16$ x $8 1/4$
A	1	Flat Head Wood Screw	$1 1/2$ x 10
B	15	Brads	1 x 18
C	6	Flat Head Wood Screws	1 x 8
D	1	Flat Head Wood Screw	$1 1/4$ x 8
E	4	Flat Head Wood Screws	$3/4$ x 8
F	6	Brads	$1 1/4$ x 18
G	4	Flat Head Wood Screws	$1 1/4$ x 8
H	9	Brads	$1 1/4$ x 18
I	8	Flat Head Wood Screws	$1 1/4$ x 8
J	7	Flat Head Wood Screws	$1 1/4$ x 10
K	16	Flat Head Wood Screws	$1 1/4$ x 10
L	1 pair	H Surface Hinges	3
M	2	Porcelain Knobs	$7/8$
N	1	Friction Latch	small

Colonial Corner Table

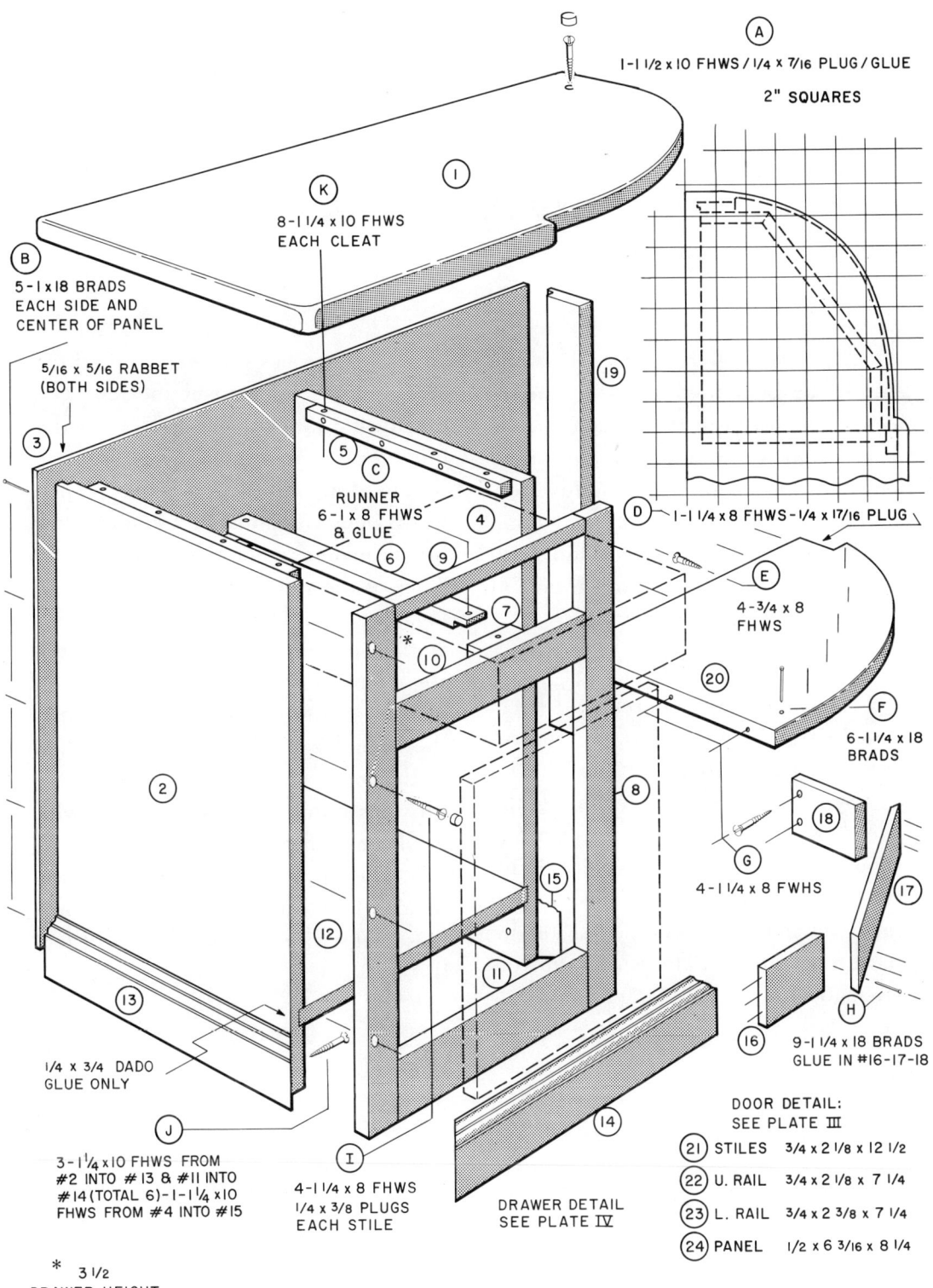

11. Colonial Corner Table

12. Tiled Coffee Table

HERE IS ANOTHER addition to the coffee table collection. This one can be individualized by the selection of tiles to fit the personal taste. The design is enhanced by the turned legs that add greatly to the hardy look. The drawers are excellent for storing playing cards, coasters, cocktail napkins, cigarettes, matches and a host of other living room essentials.

CONSTRUCTION NOTES

The first major step should be to turn the legs and then to cut the mortises in them for the skirts, see Plate VI, Fig. 4. Complete the frame including the stretchers. Note that the drawer frame is made up of five separate pieces to insure square drawer openings. Match the grain on the end stiles. See Plate IV for drawer runner details. The drawers are made last.

The tiles rest on ½" plywood which in turn lies on cleats around the inside of the opening of the top. The tiles in the table shown here were *dry fitted*, that is no cementing or grouting was used to hold them in place. When this is done care must be taken to allow for shrinkage cross grain during dry times of the year making the tile opening narrower. The finished dimensions of the opening are important and the slight looseness of the tiles is not enough to detract from appearance. The table shown had 3/32" allowed for contraction of the top cross grain in dry weather. Obviously this problem will vary with local conditions.

The top is pegged as shown for the typical hand made appearance. For those not wishing to use pegs, see Plate II, Fig. 2.

Tiled Coffee Table

Bill of Materials

PART	QUANTITY	DESCRIPTION	DIMENSION
1	10	Ceramic Tiles	*1/4 x 6 x 6
2	1	Top Insert	1/2 x 12 x 30 (plywood)
3	2	Top Edges	1 5/8 x 4 1/2 x 44
4	2	Top Ends	1 5/8 x 12 x 7
5	2	Insert Cleats (end)	5/8 x 5/8 x 12
6	2	Insert Cleats (side)	5/8 x 5/8 x 28 3/4
7	4	Legs	2 3/4 x 2 3/4 x 15 1/4
8	1	Rear Skirt	3/4 x 4 5/8 x 28 1/4
9	2	End Skirts	3/4 x 4 5/8 x 14 3/4
10	2	Drawer Runners	3/4 x 11/16 x 16 3/4
11	4	Support Blocks	3/4 x 3/4 x 1 1/2
12	1	Upper Drawer Rail	1/2 x 3/4 x 28 1/4
13	2	Drawer Stiles	3/4 x 2 1/8 x 3 1/8
14	1	Lower Drawer Rail	1 x 3/4 x 28 1/4
15	1	Center Drawer Rail	1 x 3/4 x 3 1/8
16	2	End Leg Stretchers	1 3/8 x 2 3/4 x 14 3/4
17	1	Center Leg Stretcher	1 3/8 x 2 3/4 x 30 3/8
A	18	Brads	1 x 18
B	8	Flat Head Wood Screws	2 1/2 x 10
C	14	Flat Head Wood Screws	1 x 8
D	12	Flat Head Wood Screws	1 x 8
E	2	Wooden Knobs	1 dia.

* Obtain tiles before cutting top (see text).

Tiled Coffee Table

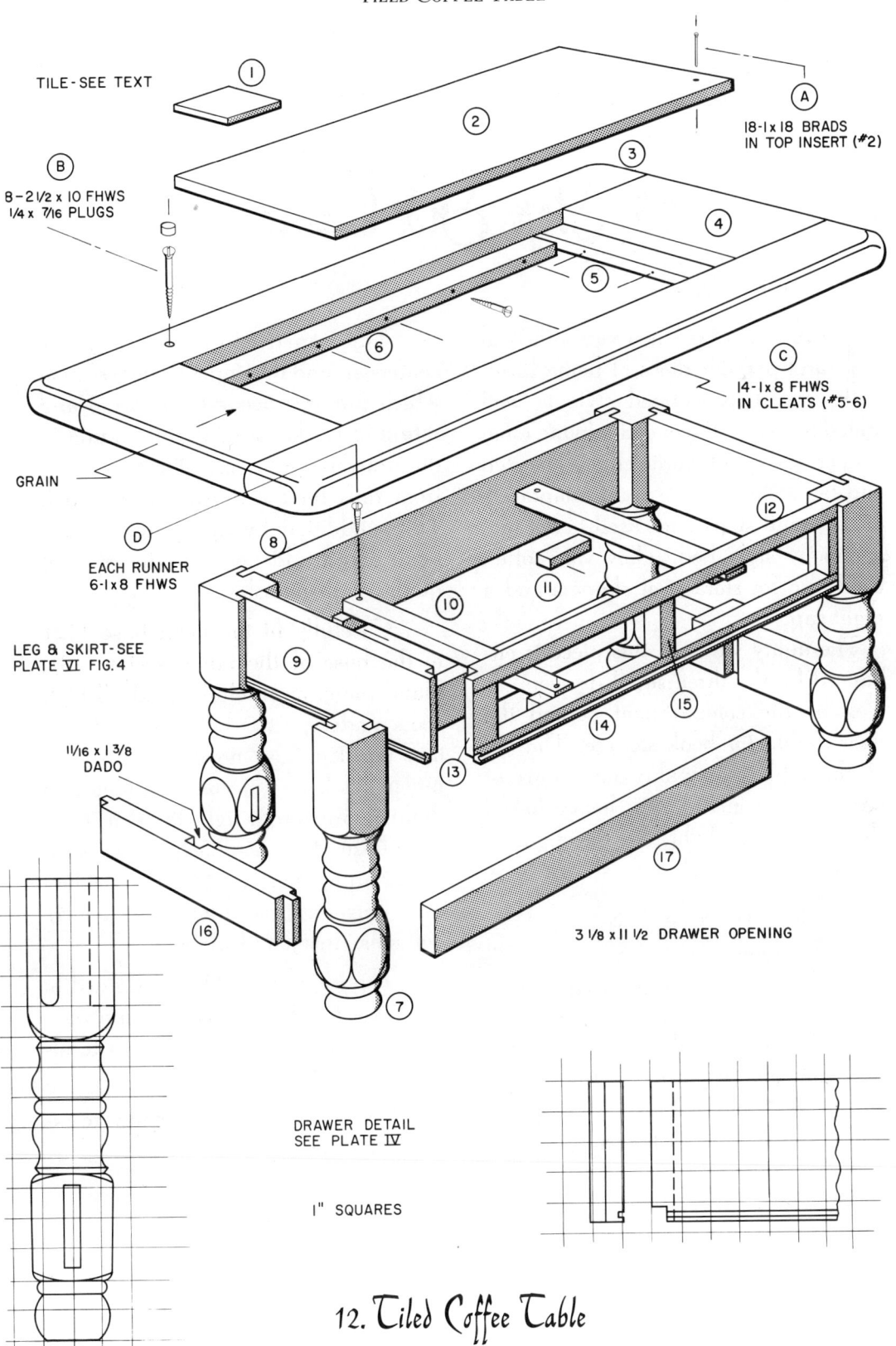

12. Tiled Coffee Table

13. Step End Table

THE END TABLE is a very practical and popular piece of home furniture. This stepped style is well suited for use at the end of a living room sofa or next to a favorite chair. The step end table shown here is an adaptation of the small steps once used to get into a canopy style bed. They were often used also for storage of slippers and a night cap.

The utility value of this piece is enhanced by the three small drawers, as well by the compartment behind the door usable for book storage. The top of the table is suitable for lamps of various sizes including a heavy based ship's running light, or the figurine planter and milk glass as shown here.

CONSTRUCTION NOTES

The dimensions given are for 3/4" stock. Those who like the rugged look characteristic of this style, and can obtain the thicker stock, could make the following changes: use 7/8" stock for parts 4, 6, 7 and 8; Use 1 1/8" stock for part 1 and 1 3/8" stock for part 12.

The construction of this piece centers around the upper storage section which requires accurate squaring and fitting of stock, especially the fitting of the drawers and door. Dovetailing the front rails for the drawers is optional. This is additional work, though not difficult and it adds much to the effect of quality craftsmanship.

Carefully fit the main base (12) to the base of the upper section (8). Hand plane or carefully sand all high spots under part 8 before screwing it into position. Use no glue. This area under this base (8) could be hollowed slightly to insure a tight fit even if the main base (12) should expand or warp some. Antiquing, (see Step 6 of the lacquer finishing procedure in Section 3) will make this joint look better.

The upper top (1) is not glued to the lower top (2) nor is the main base (12) glued to the frame. This is to allow for shrinkage.

Further construction details are explained in Section 5.

Step End Table

Bill of Materials

PART	QUANTITY	DESCRIPTION	DIMENSION
1	1	Upper Top	3/4 x 13 1/2 x 19 1/2
2	1	Lower Top	3/4 x 11 11/16 x 17
3	1	Back Panel	1/4 x 11 1/2 x 17 1/2 pine plywood
4	2	End Panels	3/4 x 11 1/2 x 12
5	4	Drawer Runners	3/4 x 3/4 x 10
6	2	Front Rails	3/4 x 1 x 8 3/4
7	1	Center Panel	3/4 x 10 1/2 x 11 11/16
8	1	Base	3/4 x 11 11/16 x 17
9	2	Front/Rear Skirts	3/4 x 5 1/2 x 14 1/4
10	2	Side Skirts	3/4 x 5 1/2 x 23 1/2
11	4	Legs	2 3/4 x 2 3/4 x 10 1/2
12	1	Main Base	1 1/8 x 19 1/2 x 29
13	2	Door Stiles	3/4 x 1 3/4 x 10
14	2	Door Rails	3/4 x 1 3/4 x 5 7/8
15	1	Door Panel	5/8 x 5 x 7 3/16
A	8	Brads	3/4 x 18
B	6	Flat Head Wood Screws	1 x 8
C	4	Flat Head Wood Screws	1 1/4 x 10
D	12	Flat Head Wood Screws	1 1/4 x 8
E	12	Flat Head Wood Screws	1 3/4 x 10
F	4	Flat Head Wood Screws	1 1/2 x 12
G	1 pair	Antiqued Butt Hinges	1 3/8 x 2
H	4	Porcelain Knobs	1 dia.
I	1	Friction Latch	small

Step End Table

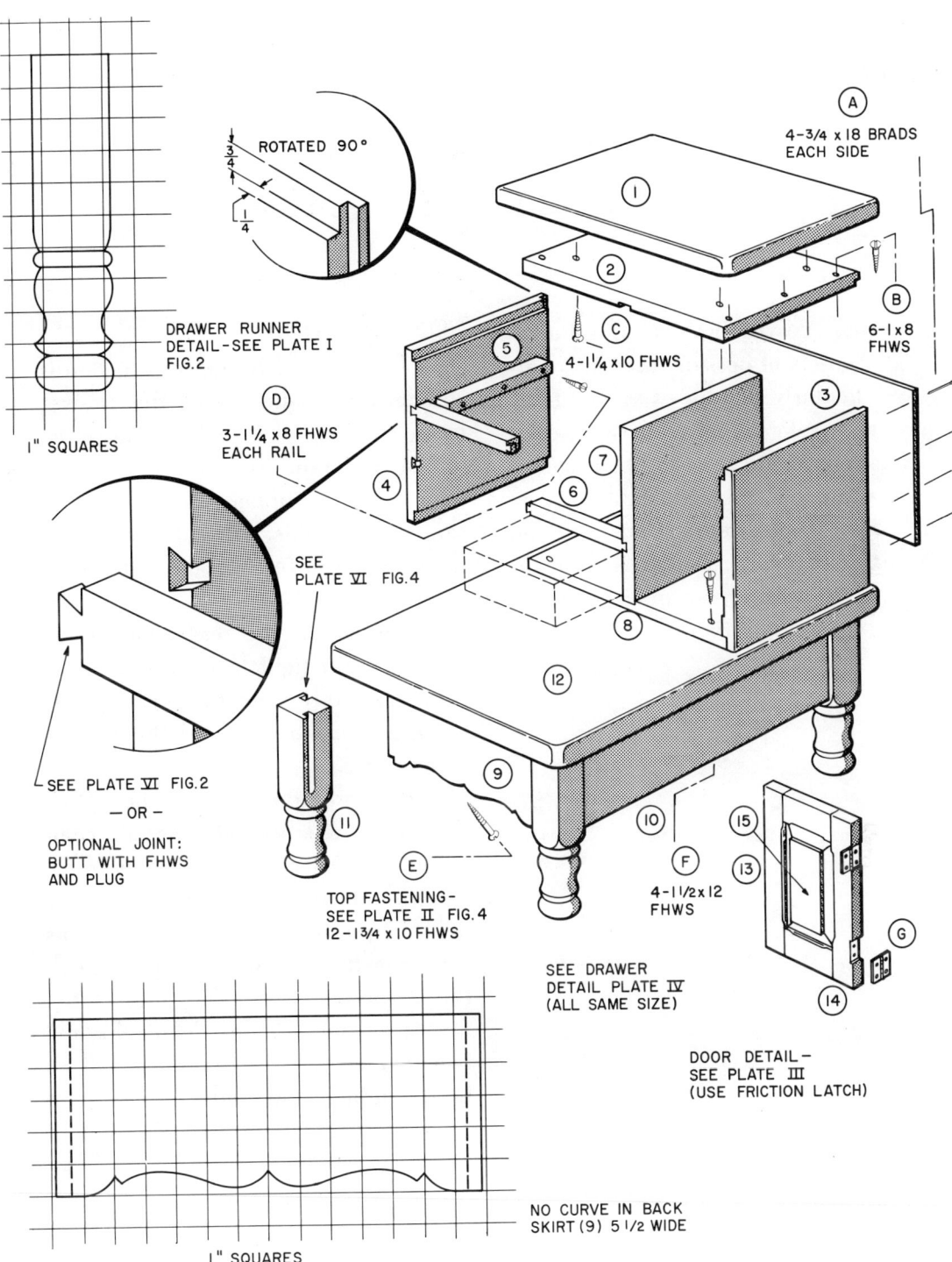

13. Step End Table

14. Towel Bar Table

THIS TOWEL BAR TABLE has a variety of possible uses. It is particularly suitable as an end table next to a sofa or between two casual living room chairs. For the bed room it makes an excellent night table next to a bed for books, radio, clock, or even for a lamp, which is high enough for reading. A further use may be in the dining room as a server.

CONSTRUCTION NOTES

The leg and frame construction is standard procedure with the drawer frame built up of 5 pieces. The center rail of this frame is made into a dado joint with the upper and lower rails simple butt joints. Glue together after shaping the lower rail and cut rabbet joints in the ends.

Square up the rear edge of the top (1) for a tight fit against the rear skirt. Carefully sand these two pieces making a smooth, blended effect at the rear corners.

Assemble the upper section (top, skirt, bars and brackets) as one complete unit. After legs and lower frame are assembled as one unit, the top is held in position with three cleats as shown in the drawing and in Plate II, Fig. 2.

See Plate IV for details for the two divided drawer fronts as well as for the runners and guides.

Towel Bar Table

Bill of Materials

PART	QUANTITY	DESCRIPTION	DIMENSION
1	1	Top	$1\frac{1}{8}$ x $16\frac{3}{4}$ x 24
2	1	Rear Skirt	$1\frac{1}{8}$ x $4\frac{1}{4}$ x 27
3	2	Towel Bars	$1\frac{1}{4}$ x $1\frac{1}{4}$ x $17\frac{3}{4}$
4	2	Front Brackets	$1\frac{1}{8}$ x $3\frac{7}{8}$ x $4\frac{1}{2}$
5	4	Legs	$2\frac{1}{4}$ x $2\frac{1}{4}$ x 23
6	2	Side Panels	$\frac{3}{4}$ x $9\frac{1}{4}$ x $14\frac{1}{8}$
7	1	Rear Panel	$\frac{3}{4}$ x $9\frac{1}{4}$ x $19\frac{1}{2}$
8	2	Stiles	$\frac{3}{4}$ x $1\frac{3}{4}$ x $6\frac{3}{4}$
9	1	Upper Rail	$\frac{3}{4}$ x $\frac{3}{4}$ x $19\frac{1}{2}$
10	1	Center Rail	$\frac{3}{4}$ x $\frac{3}{4}$ x $16\frac{1}{2}$
11	1	Lower Rail	$\frac{3}{4}$ x $1\frac{3}{4}$ x $19\frac{1}{2}$
12	2	Drawer Runners	$\frac{3}{4}$ x $1\frac{11}{16}$ x 16
13	4	Runner Supports	$\frac{3}{4}$ x $\frac{3}{4}$ x $1\frac{1}{2}$
14	2	Side Panel Cleats	$\frac{3}{4}$ x 1 x $12\frac{1}{4}$
15	1	Rear Panel Cleat	$\frac{3}{4}$ x 1 x $17\frac{3}{4}$
A	2	Flat Head Wood Screws	$1\frac{1}{2}$ x 8
B	3	Flat Head Wood Screws	$1\frac{1}{2}$ x 10
C	12	Flat Head Wood Screws	$1\frac{1}{4}$ x 10
D	12	Flat Head Wood Screws	1 x 8
E	6	Porcelain Knobs	$\frac{3}{4}$ dia.

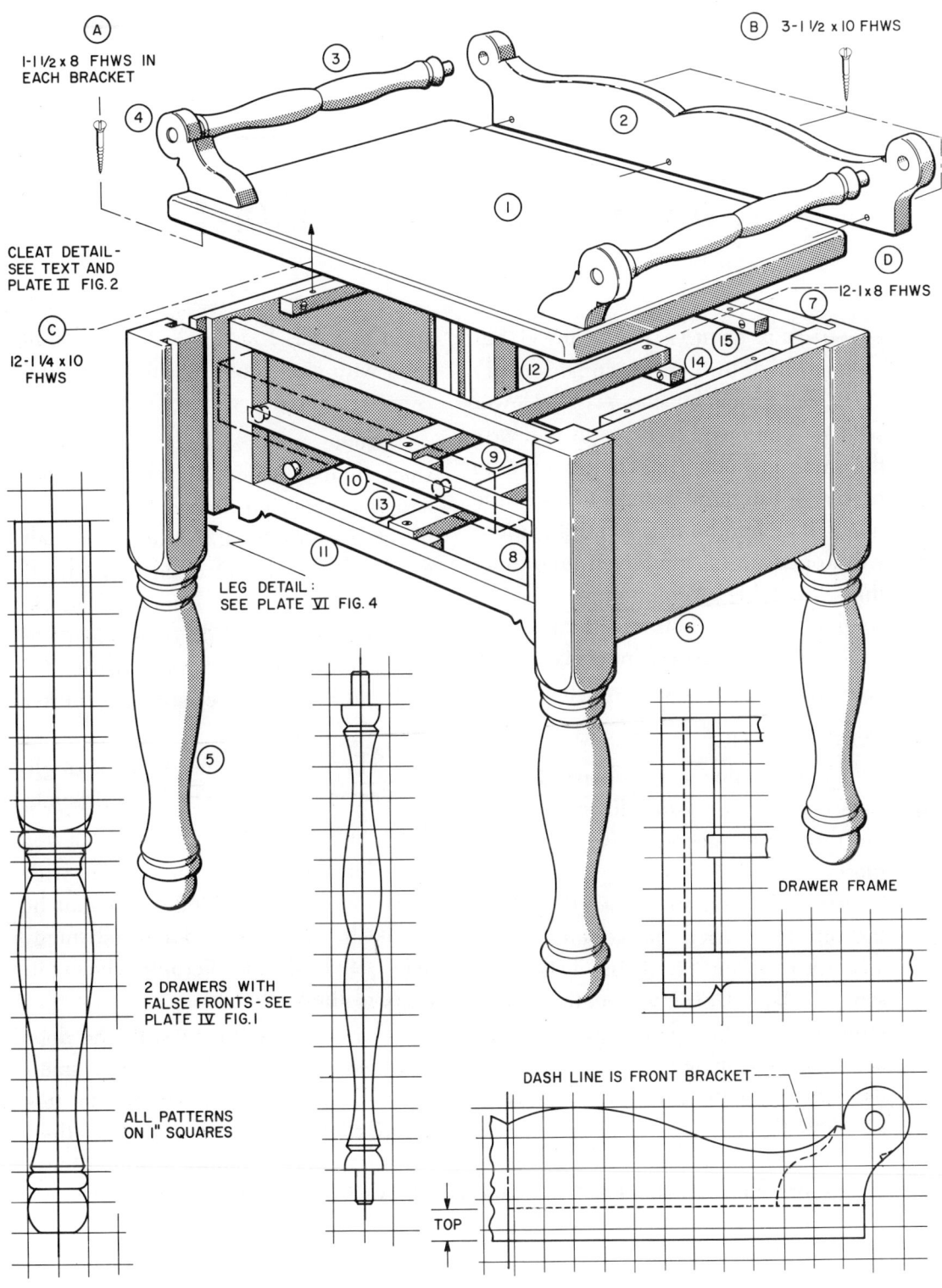

14. Towel Bar Table

15. Towel Bar Cabinet

THIS IS SIMILAR to the towel bar table, but offers considerably more room for storage in the lower section. The towel bar design is nearly the same in both. Both pieces may be placed in the same general areas in the home. It should be noted that this piece will appear to fill any given area more than the table even though they are similar in size. This is because the lower section of the cabinet cuts off any view of the floor or the wall behind it.

CONSTRUCTION NOTES

Construction can be divided into two sections, upper and lower. Assemble the upper section consisting of six pieces. The rear skirt (2) is fastened by screws (A) passing upward through the top (1). Insert turned towel bars (3) and fasten front brackets with screws (B) from underneath and a minimum of glue. The completed top assembly is fastened (after the base is assembled) to the side panels by cleats, see Plate II, Fig. 2.

The upper and lower drawer rails (7, 8) are shown with dovetail joints, see Plate VI, Fig. 2. A doweled butt joint with glue could be substituted but is not as strong.

Some may wish to use heavier stock than specified. If a heavier door is made, note that the front frame must be at least as thick as the door itself or the door will not close properly. If the door were made from 1⅛" stock, the raised panel should be increased to ¾" stock, and the top should be ⅜" wider to properly overhang the thicker front.

The drawer runner is for a single drawer with front inlaid to simulate three separate drawers.

Porcelain knobs are shown with black iron H surface hinges with matching latch. A porcelain knob and magnetic catch is an alternate choice in place of the latch.

The door is shown with the door stiles and rails molded with a small "bead and shoulder" cutter, do this before gluing the door frame together. An alternative is simply to soften these edges with garnet paper.

Towel Bar Cabinet

Bill of Materials

PART	QUANTITY	DESCRIPTION	DIMENSION
1	1	Top	$1\frac{1}{8} \times 18 \times 25\frac{1}{4}$
2	1	Rear Skirt	$1\frac{1}{8} \times 5 \times 30$
3	2	Towel Bars	$1\frac{3}{8} \times 1\frac{3}{8} \times 17\frac{5}{8}$
4	2	Front Brackets	$1\frac{1}{8} \times 4 \times 5$
5	2	End Panels	$\frac{3}{4} \times 16\frac{1}{2} \times 24$
6	2	Frame Stiles	$\frac{3}{4} \times 4 \times 24$
7	1	Top Rail	$\frac{3}{4} \times \frac{7}{8} \times 16\frac{1}{2}$
8	1	Lower Rail	$\frac{3}{4} \times \frac{7}{8} \times 16\frac{1}{2}$
9	1	Drawer Runner	$\frac{3}{4} \times \frac{11}{16} \times 16\frac{1}{2}$
10	2	Runner Supports	$\frac{3}{4} \times \frac{3}{4} \times 1\frac{1}{2}$
11	2	Side Panel Cleats	$\frac{3}{4} \times 1 \times 15$
12	1	Back Panel	$\frac{1}{4} \times 23\frac{1}{8} \times 24$ pine plywood
13	1	Bottom	$\frac{3}{4} \times 16\frac{1}{2} \times 22\frac{3}{4}$
14	2	Door Stiles	$\frac{3}{4} \times 2\frac{5}{8} \times 14\frac{1}{2}$
15	1	Upper Door Rail	$\frac{3}{4} \times 2\frac{5}{8} \times 12\frac{3}{4}$
16	1	Lower Door Rail	$\frac{3}{4} \times 2\frac{3}{4} \times 12\frac{3}{4}$
17	1	Door Panel	$\frac{5}{8} \times 9\frac{1}{2} \times 10\frac{7}{8}$
A	4	Flat Head Wood Screws	$1\frac{3}{4} \times 10$
B	2	Flat Head Wood Screws	$1\frac{3}{4} \times 10$
C	6	Flat Head Wood Screws	1×8
D	6	Flat Head Wood Screws	$1\frac{1}{4} \times 8$
E	18	Flat Head Wood Screws	$1\frac{1}{2} \times 10$
F	1 pair	H Surface Hinges	3"
G	1	Latch	small (match hinges)
H	3	Porcelain Knobs	$\frac{3}{4}$

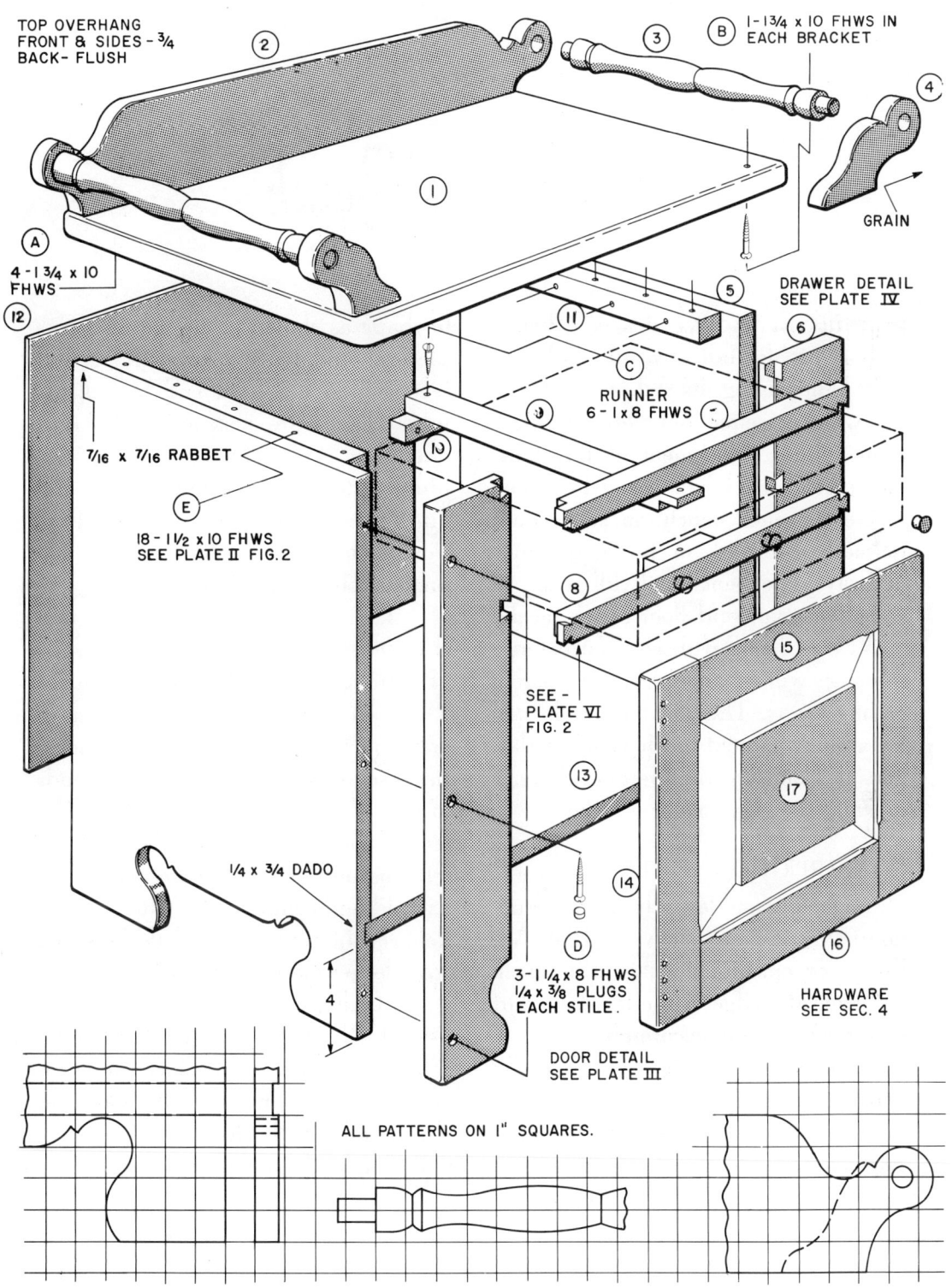

15. Towel Bar Cabinet

16. Deacons' Bench

THIS ATTRACTIVE deacon's bench is highly indicative of hardy colonial living. Its style is similar to the windsor settee but with far more rugged lines. Placement of this four-foot piece may be in the living room where a small couch or sofa could normally be used, or in an entrance hallway. The bench will fill a six to eight foot wall and floor space nicely.

For a home with colonial exterior this piece will enhance a veranda, porch, or breezeway. This location might call for a black painted finish (with medallions or Pennsylvania German design) to stand the elements of weather.

CONSTRUCTION NOTES

The legs and lower frame construction is the same as shown in Plate VI, Fig. 4, except that the skirt is set back ½" from the edge of the leg. Cut skirt ends and leg taper accurately.

Cut the heart design out of the ends before gluing up the end panels to save tedious cutting. Cut the hand grip out of square stock, file and sand to shape as shown in the pattern. This piece should have a hand-shaped effect. Soften the front end to indicate wear. These are fastened with brads and glue. An addition might be two plugs without screws, the brads and glue are sufficient. Place the plugs 1½" from each end of the hand grip at 30° angle as shown in the pattern.

The assembled end and back unit is fastened to the seat with 17 screws (B) from underneath, which includes 3 into each end piece. Apply glue to only the front third of the end pieces because pressure against the back tends to raise the front of the end piece. The rear of the end piece and the back are left unglued, and therefore are free to expand and contract. The fifteen shank holes in the rear areas should be about $\frac{1}{16}$" larger than the gage of the screws.

Finally, the seat is fastened to the assembled leg section using 17 similar screws (B). These are placed 60° upward from the inside of the skirts as shown in Plate II, Fig. 4. Use 3 at ends, 6 in front, and 5 in the rear.

Bill of Materials

PART	QUANTITY	DESCRIPTION	DIMENSION
1	1	Upper Back Rail	1 3/8 x 5 x 45
2	1	Lower Back Rail	1 3/8 x 3 3/4 x 45
3	1	Seat	1 3/8 x 16 1/2 x 48
4	2	End Panels	1 3/8 x 16 3/4 x 20
5	4	Legs	2 1/2 x 2 1/2 x 15 1/2
6	2	Lower Skirts	1 1/8 x 5 x 42 1/2
7	2	End Skirts	1 1/8 x 5 x 10 7/8
8	13	Spindles	3/4 dia. x 12 1/4
9	2	Hand Grips	2 x 2 x 7
A	4	Flat Head Wood Screws	1 3/4 x 12
B	34	Flat Head Wood Screws	2 1/2 x 12
C	8	Brads	1 1/4 x 18
D	4	Plugs (optional)	1/4 x 1/2

Deacons' Bench

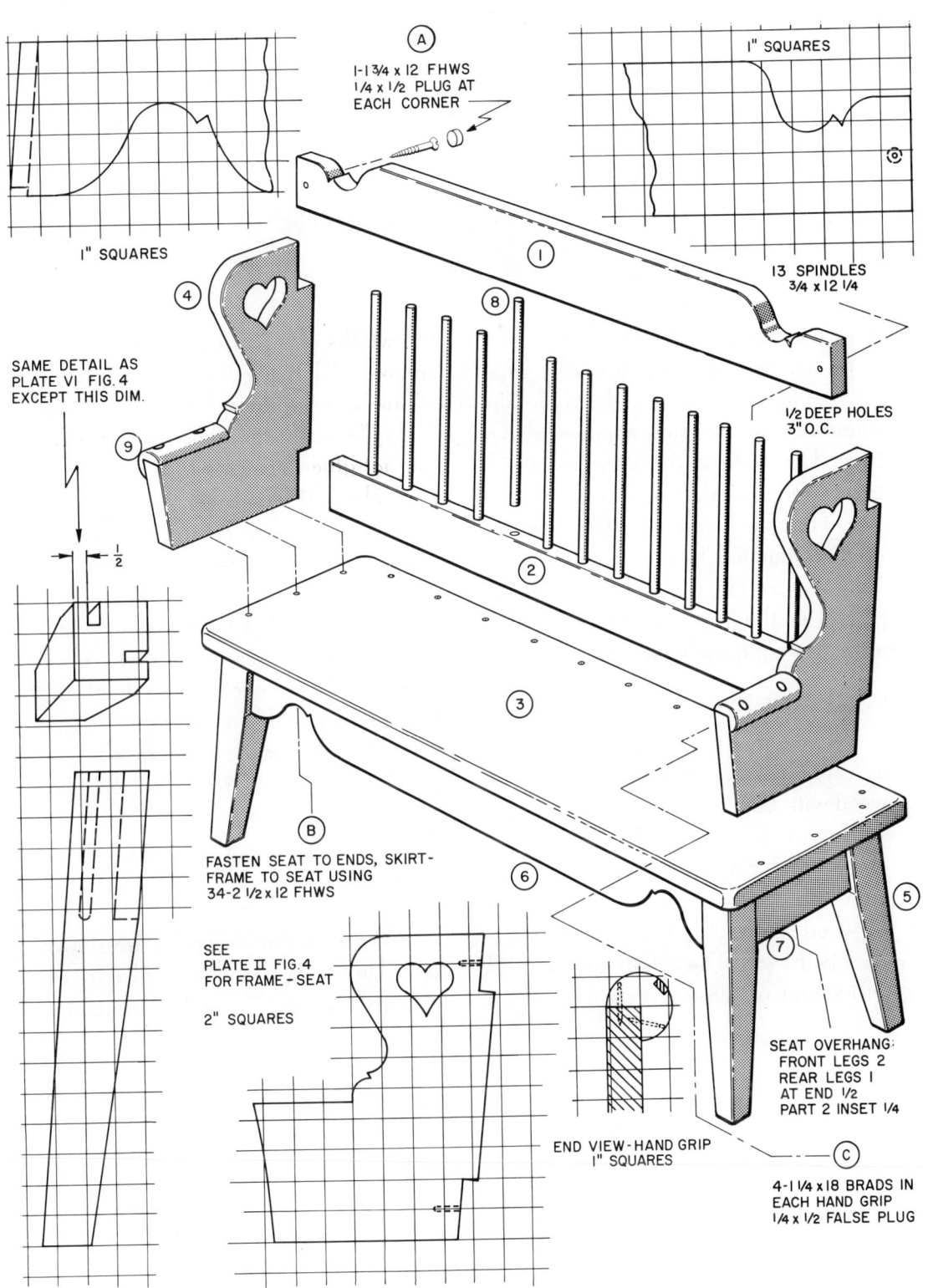

16. Deacons' Bench

17. Hutch Table

THE GRACEFUL DESIGN of this table speaks for itself especially when placed in such a desirable surrounding as the bay window shown here. This style of furniture was sometimes used as a combination chair-table.

This piece was adapted from the original that may be seen in the Morgan Museum at Hartford, Conn. When placed in the "up" position it is most attractive against a wall area.

CONSTRUCTION NOTES

The top requires some special care in construction. Use straight grained wood with little or no warp. Glue up the top from pieces 6" to 8" in width with the annual rings alternated and the grain matched. The drawing indicates 11 wood screws (E, EE) fastening the cleat to the top. The actual number and positioning of these screws depend on the widths of the pieces in the top. End screws (EE) are shorter. Drill the shank holes for the screws approximately $3/32$" oversize to allow for shrinkage. *Do not glue the cleats to the top.*

The end panels mortise and tenon joints should allow for the distance between tenons to change with humidity conditions.

See Plate I, Fig. 1 — note where a split could occur. The two wood screws (C) in each tenon hold this joint so the panel can expand.

The elongated holes in the end panels (3) are 2" from the top. The holes in the cleats (2) are $2\frac{1}{2}$" from the top. The difference provides clearance to prevent binding when the top is lowered.

Wooden drawer knobs are shown here. However, porcelain knobs are also popular—use $1\frac{1}{8}$" or $1\frac{1}{4}$" diameter.

Bill of Materials

PART	QUANTITY	DESCRIPTION	DIMENSION
1	1	Top	1 x 40 dia.
2	2	Cleats	1⅛ x 3 x 36
3	2	End Panels	⅞ x 13⅝ x 26¾
4	1	Top Shelf	1 x 13⅝ x 16¾
5	2	False Drawer Fronts	¾ x 4¼ x 16
6	4	Drawer Rails	¾ x 1 x 16¾
7	4	Drawer Runners	¾ x 1¼ x 11¼
8	4	Cleat Knobs	1⅜ x 1⅜ x 5
9	1	Stretcher	1¼ x 2¾ x 19⅜
10	2	Feet	2½ x 2¾ x 23
A	12	Brads	1½ x 18
B	12	Flat Head Wood Screws	1¼ x 8
C	8	Flat Head Wood Screws	2½ x 8
D	2	Flat Head Wood Screws	2½ x 10
E	18	Flat Head Wood Screws	2¾ x 12
EE	4	Flat Head Wood Screws	2 x 12 (for ends)
F	4	Drawer Knobs	1⅛ or 1¼ dia.

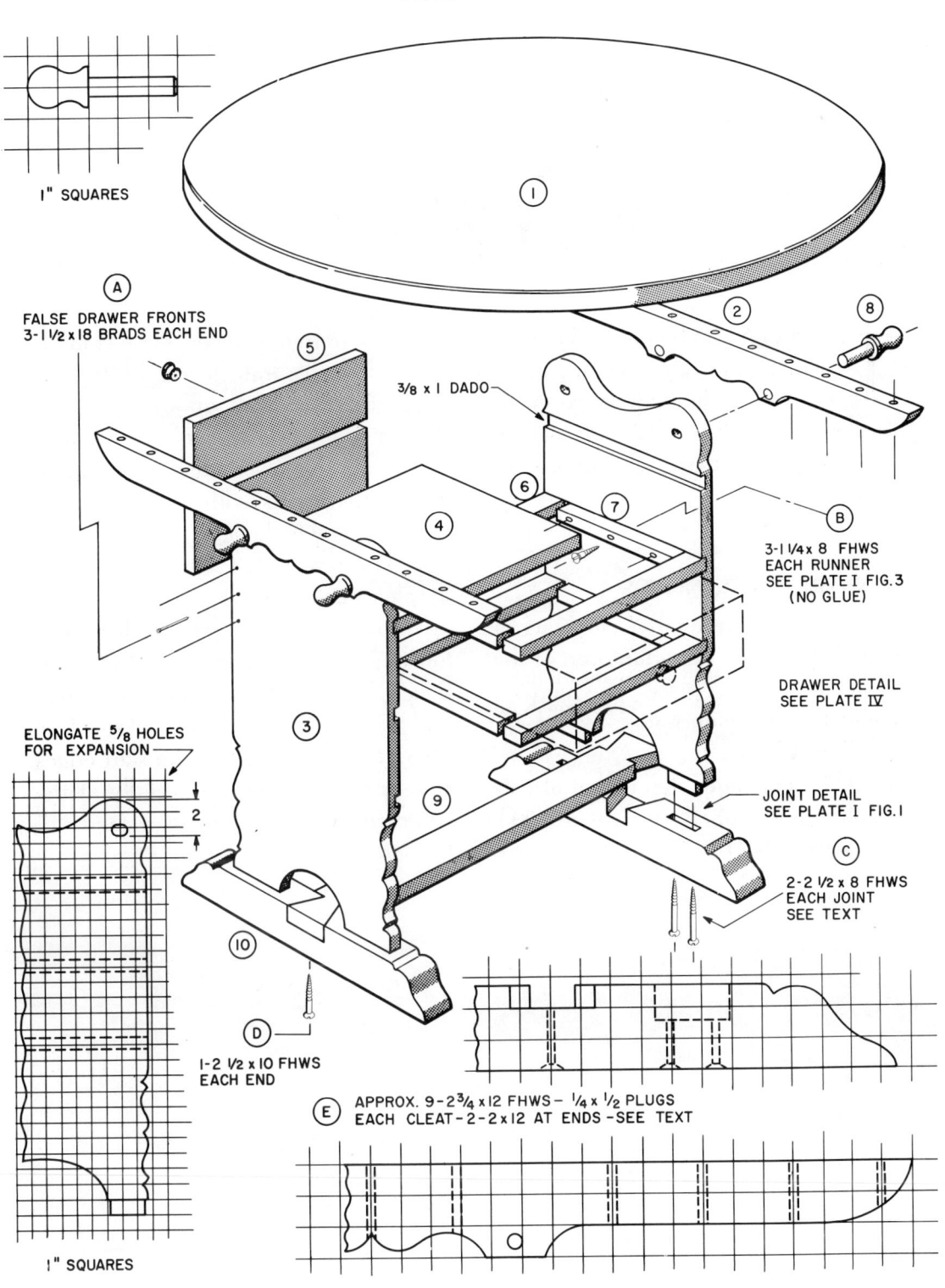

17. Hutch Table

18. Night Table

THIS TABLE can be placed between twin beds to hold a reading lamp, clock, or radio with space in the drawer for small objects. It is an excellent piece for those who desire the beauty of lathe-turned legs.

CONSTRUCTION NOTES

Accurate turning and mortising of the four legs is an important part of the construction of this piece. The mortises should be $3/8''$ wide and $1\ 3/16''$ deep. See Plate VI, Fig. 4.

The next major step is that of cutting the upper panels (6, 7, 9, 10, 11) and lower rails (14, 15) to make up the frame. The front drawer frame is made up of four separate pieces to give an accurately squared opening for the drawer front. Cut a $1/8'' \times 1/8''$ dado $3/16''$ from the lower edge of all panels. Soften these cuts with abrasive paper before gluing to the legs.

The lower slats may be fastened in place using brads and glue. They are brought out even with the legs. The top and skirt assembly should be completed, but not fastened until the drawer and its runner are fitted in place. Use abrasive paper to blend the skirt edges (3) to the rear skirt, especially at the two corners. The top should extend $3/4''$ beyond the legs.

Night Table

Bill of Materials

PART	QUANTITY	DESCRIPTION	DIMENSION
1	2	Side Skirts	$3/4 \times 3 1/4 \times 11 1/8$
2	1	Rear Skirt	$3/4 \times 5 \times 21$
3	2	Side Skirt Edges	$1/2 \times 3/4 \times 6 1/4$
4	1	Top	*$7/8 \times 17 1/2 \times 21 3/4$
5	4	Legs	$2 1/4 \times 2 1/4 \times 22 1/4$
6	2	Side Panels	$3/4 \times 6 3/8 \times 13$
7	1	Rear Panel	$3/4 \times 6 3/8 \times 17 1/4$
8	4	Cleats	$3/4 \times 1 \times 11$
9	1	Upper Rail	$3/4 \times 1 \times 17 1/4$
10	1	Lower Rail	$3/4 \times 1 1/8 \times 17 1/4$
11	2	Stiles	$3/4 \times 1 3/4 \times 4 1/4$
12	2	Runner Supports	$3/4 \times 3/4 \times 1 1/2$
13	1	Drawer Runner	$3/4 \times {}^{11}/_{16} \times 14 1/8$
14	2	Front/Rear Rails	$3/4 \times 2 \times 17 1/4$
15	2	Side Rails	$3/4 \times 2 \times 13$
16, 20	2	Outside Slats	$1/2 \times 2 1/4 \times 15 3/4$
17-19	3	Center Slats	$1/2 \times 3 {}^{13}/_{16} \times 20 1/4$
A	6	Brads	$1 1/4 \times 18$
B	24	Flat Head Wood Screws	$1 1/4 \times 10$
C	2	Flat Head Wood Screws	$1 1/2 \times 8$
D	8	Flat Head Wood Screws	$1 1/4 \times 8$
E	6	Flat Head Wood Screws	1×8
F	20	Brads	$1 1/2 \times 16$
G	2	Porcelain Knob	$7/8$ dia.

* $7/8$ Recommended, $3/4$ Acceptable

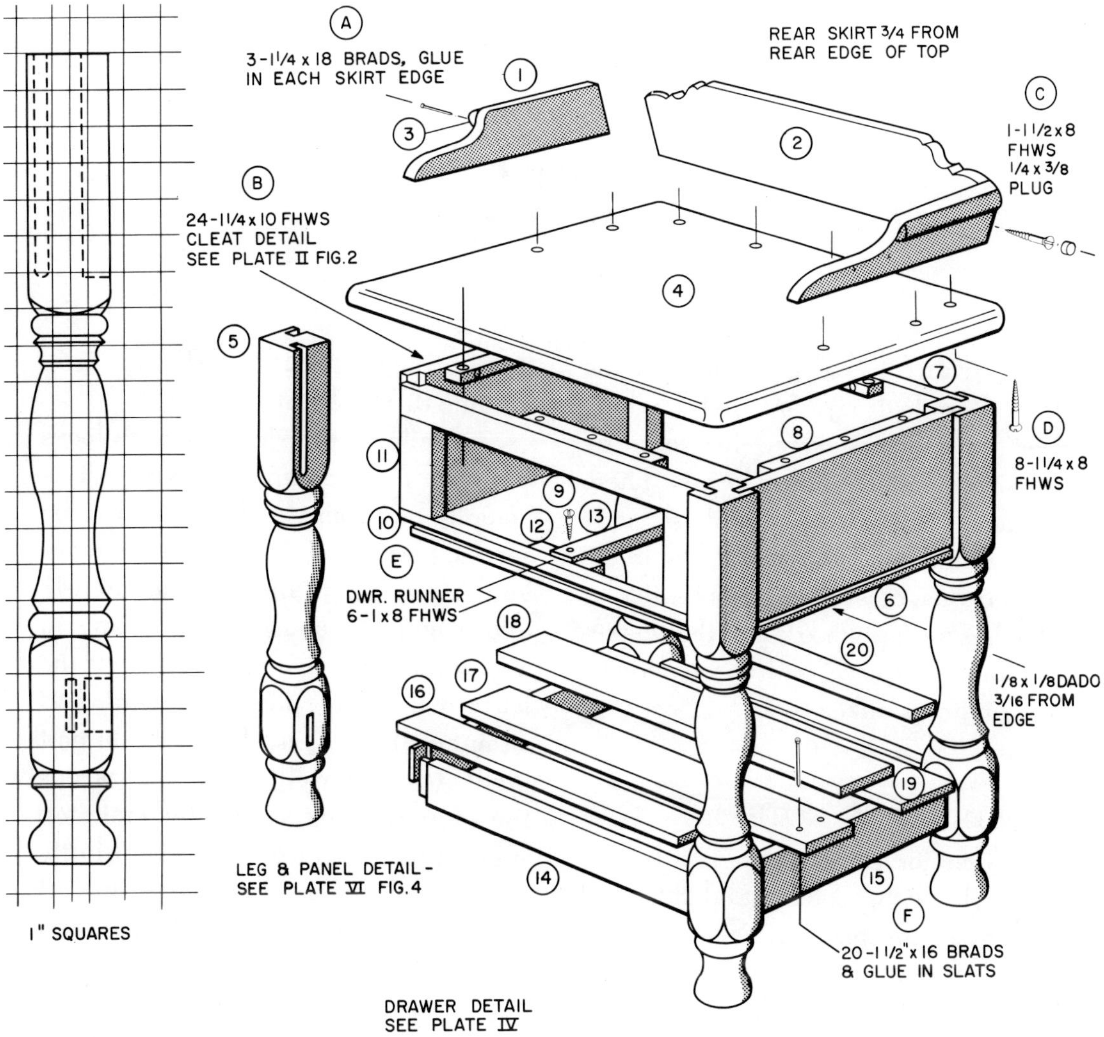

Night Table

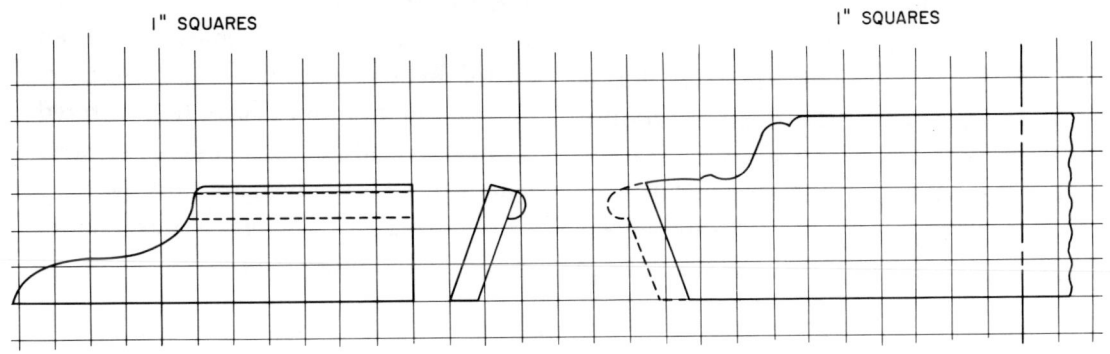

18. Night Table

19. Tripod Table

BOTH THE tripod pedestal and the drop leaf top are styles which have been favored for years by craftsmen and furniture lovers. There are many variations of this basic style such as the solid top that tilts, or the popular "pie crust" top. This particular table has a simplified design that makes it a popular piece with professionals and amateurs alike.

CONSTRUCTION NOTES

A major construction problem of this table is the cutting and fitting of the legs to the pedestal. See Plate V, Fig. 2 for a method of cutting the mortises in the pedestal. An angle of 20° is cut on the shoulders of the leg tenons so they will join the arc of the pedestal for a tight fit.

The rule joint for the table top is best made with standard matching cutter bits for router-shapers. When fastening the top to the main top support (3) do not use glue to allow for expansion. If there is slight warping of the drop leafs see Plate VI, Fig. 3 regarding this problem.

While the drop leaf assembly looks complex in the exploded view, it is actually quite simple. The parts can be seen in position in the view at the upper left. A pin (7) in the leaf support (4) allows it to be grasped for sliding in and out. A drop leaf stop (5) keeps the leaf from being pushed inward and straining the hinges. The leaf support guide (6) (as well as Stop 5) keeps the support riding against the main top support as it is pushed back and forth. To keep the rear of the leaf support from dropping downward when pushed in, a brad (G) is driven as shown to hold it up against the table top. The feather blocks (8) allow fine adjustment of the drop leaves so they will be exactly level with the main top when in the up position. The $3/16''$ thickness is suggested but may have to be altered in the final fitting. Assemble these parts carefully. Also make sure that the drop leaves are in a true vertical position before fastening the stop blocks.

Tripod Table

Bill of Materials

PART	QUANTITY	DESCRIPTION	DIMENSION
1	2	Drop Leaves	1 1/8 x 9 3/4 x 32 1/2
2	1	Main Top	1 1/8 x 14 3/8 x 32 1/2
3	1	Main Top Support	1 1/8 x 5 1/4 x 13 1/2
4	2	Leaf Supports	3/4 x 1 5/8 x 13
5	4	Drop Leaf Stops	1 x 1 1/4 x 2 1/2
6	2	Leaf Support Guides	1/2 x 1 x 1
7	2	Leaf Support Pins	3/8 x 3/4
8	2	Feather Blocks	3/16 x 5/8 x 1 3/4
9	1	Pedestal	4 3/8 x 4 3/8 x 15
10	3	Legs	1 3/8 x 4 x 14 1/4
A	2 pair	Hinges	1 1/2 x 4
B	3	Flat Head Wood Screws	2 1/2 x 12
C	8	Flat Head Wood Screws	1 3/4 x 10
D	6	Flat Head Wood Screws	1 x 8
E	2	Round Head Wood Screws	1 1/4 x 10
F	2	Flat Washers	1/4
G	2	Brads	1 1/2 x 14
H	2	Brads	3/4 x 18

TRIPOD TABLE

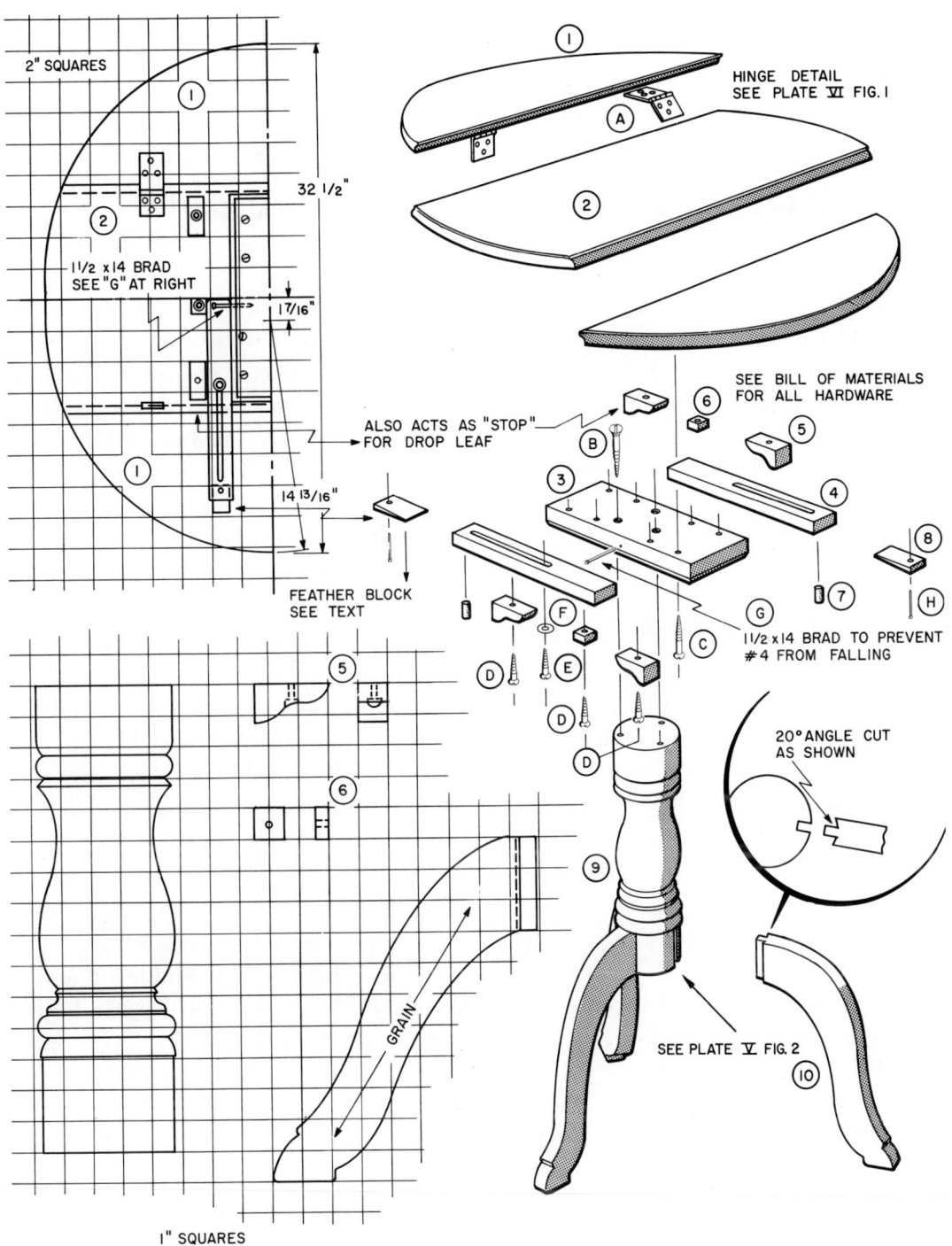

19. Tripod Table

20. Drop Leaf Rudder Table

THIS UNUSUAL TABLE is another of the popular and versatile drop leaf styles. The size allows for a variety of settings in most homes: as a table with one or both leaves raised, as an end table at the end of a living room sofa, or as a server in a dining room.

CONSTRUCTION NOTES

The first unit assembled is that of the ends and feet. The two pieces are glued up to make each end panel. Carefully cut the drawer opening before gluing up that end. The feet are fastened to the ends with a mortise and tenon joint and three flat head wood screws. Glue only at the center and elongate the mortises slightly to allow for expansion.

Position the skirts (4) and rails (5) but *do not add stretcher yet*.

The center piece of the top (1) can be fastened as shown in Plate II, Fig. 4, using 12 flat head wood screws (B) and no glue. Another choice is the pegged effect shown in Plate II, Fig. 3, using 10 screws (1½" x 8), 3 on each side and 2 on each end.

Next fit the wings (8) to the top and to the stretcher. These parts should be assembled dry as a check before final gluing. Glue and brad the upper wing supports (10) to the top. Then glue the upper dowels (11) into the wings. Insert into support.

The lower dowel rod (12) is pushed up through the ⅜" hole in the stretcher. Insert a flat washer under the wing to take up any play and to allow smoother movement. A spot of glue holds the dowel in the stretcher.

The feather block (13) allows leveling of the leaves with the main top. The feather blocks are listed as 3/16" thick but vary as needed. The stop block (14) prevents the wings from being pushed beyond the center.

The rule joint on the table top and leaves can be made with the standard matching cutter bits.

If 1⅛" stock is not available the table can be made from ⅞" or even ¾" stock. However, a ¾" top is rather thin for proper proportion.

The hinges can vary in size and need not be in the butterfly shape. Suppliers are indicated in Section 6.

Drop Leaf Rudder Table

Bill of Materials

PART	QUANTITY	DESCRIPTION	DIMENSION
1	1	Top	1 1/8 x 15 x 29 1/4
2	2	Drop Leaves	1 1/8 x 9 1/4 x 26 1/4
3	2	Ends	1 1/8 x 11 1/2 x 20 7/8
4	2	Skirts	3/4 x 4 3/4 x 18 5/8
5	1	Drawer Rail	1 1/8 x 1 1/8 x 9
6	2	Lower Rails	1 1/8 x 3 x 20 3/8
7	1	Stretcher	3/4 x 2 1/2 x 16 3/8
8	2	Wings	3/4 x 7 3/8 x 15 1/2
9	2	Feet	2 1/2 x 3 x 19 1/2
10	2	Wing Supports	3/8 x 3/4 x 1
11	2	Upper Dowel Rods	3/8 x 5/8
12	2	Lower Dowel Rods	3/8 x 1 1/4
13	2	Feather Blocks	3/16 x 3/4 x 1 1/2
14	2	Stop Blocks	3/8 x 3/8 x 1
15	1	Drawer Runner	11/16 x 3/4 x 18 1/2
16	2	Runner Supports	3/4 x 3/4 x 1 1/2
A	6	Brads	3/4 x 18
B	12	Flat Head Wood Screws	1 1/4 x 8
C	2	Flat Head Wood Screws	1 1/2 x 8
D	4	Brads	1 x 18
E	6	Flat Head Wood Screws	1 x 8
F	8	Flat Head Wood Screws	1 1/2 x 8
G	6	Flat Head Wood Screws	2 1/4 x 8
H	2 pair	Butterfly Hinges	1 3/4 x 2 (see text)
I	1	Porcelain Knob	1 1/4 dia.

Drop Leaf Rudder Table

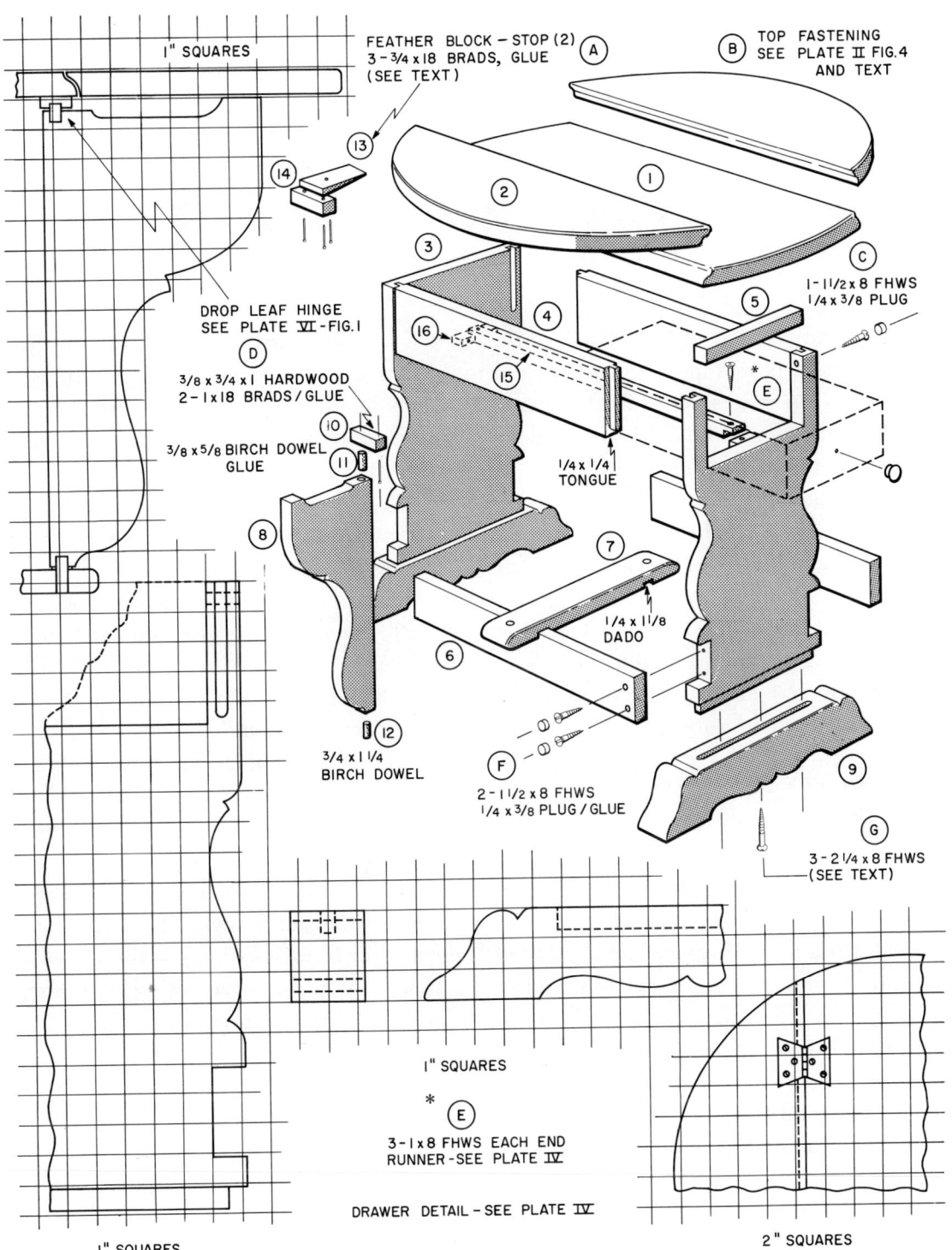

20. Drop Leaf Rudder Table

21. Dough Box End Table

Borrowing from the kitchen of the early days, this design utilizes one of the mainstays of food preparation — the dough box. It was used for storing dough for baked products.

Today the dough box of the colonial kitchen has been moved into the living room for use as an end table. The height is good because it is about the same as that of the arm of most sofas. This piece makes an excellent mate for the step end table, to be used at the opposite end of a sofa.

CONSTRUCTION NOTES

Care must be taken in laying out the proper angle on the side and end skirts. See Plate VI, Fig. 4. Parts 1, 2, 4, 5, and 6 can be made from ⅞ or 1 inch stock if this heavier look is desired and the thicker pine is obtainable. Dimensions given here are for a ⅜" deep rabbet in ends (4) in ¾" stock.

The rabbet cuts in the end pieces are made on the circular saw. It is also possible to simply butt these joints. In either method make certain that the base (6) extends at least ⅝" beyond the main body at the sides and ends.

The outward tilt of parts 1 and 5 creates a triangular gap at the corners when fitted to the top and base. File, sand, or bevel cut the high edges for an accurate fit.

Make a dry fit and mark all legs (after turning) carefully and make sure the leg angle is cut in the proper direction and angle in relation to the skirts (7-8). Some may prefer to glue the legs and skirts and then belt sand or disk sand the high points to the proper angle. *Use extreme care in doing this.*

The base (6) is fastened to the main body (4, 5) with 14 screws (D) before the base is fastened to the legs and skirts. Allow for angle of parts 4 and 5. The base is then fastened to the frame with four screws (C) into the legs. Glue is not necessary — the screws often cause a "squeeze out" that stains the wood. Antiquing helps to fill these joints, see Step 6 in Section 3.

The cleat (3) prevents possible warping of the lid. Use no glue to allow for expansion.

Use hinges with an antiqued finish for the best effect. However, flat black paint on steel hinges can be used.

Dough Box End Table

Bill of Materials

PART	QUANTITY	DESCRIPTION	DIMENSION
1	1	Stationary Top	$3/4 \times 18 5/8 \times 14 1/2$
2	1	Movable Top	$3/4 \times 18 5/8 \times 11 5/8$
3	1	Cleat	$1 1/8 \times 2 \times 13 1/2$
4	2	End Panels	$3/4 \times 10 1/2 \times 16 13/16$
5	2	Side Panels	$3/4 \times 10 1/2 \times 22 3/4$
6	1	Base	$3/4 \times 13 3/4 \times 20 7/16$
7	2	Side Skirts	$3/4 \times 3 3/8 \times 17$
8	2	End Skirts	$3/4 \times 3 3/8 \times 10 1/2$
9	4	Legs	$2 5/16 \times 2 5/16 \times 10 3/4$
A	14	Brads	$1 1/2 \times 16$
B	4	Flat Head Wood Screws	$1 1/2 \times 12$
C	4	Flat Head Wood Screws	$1 1/4 \times 12$
D	14	Flat Head Wood Screws	$1 1/2 \times 8$
E	12	Flat Head Wood Screws	$3/4 \times 8$
F	1 pair	Antiqued Butt Hinges	$1 3/8 \times 2$

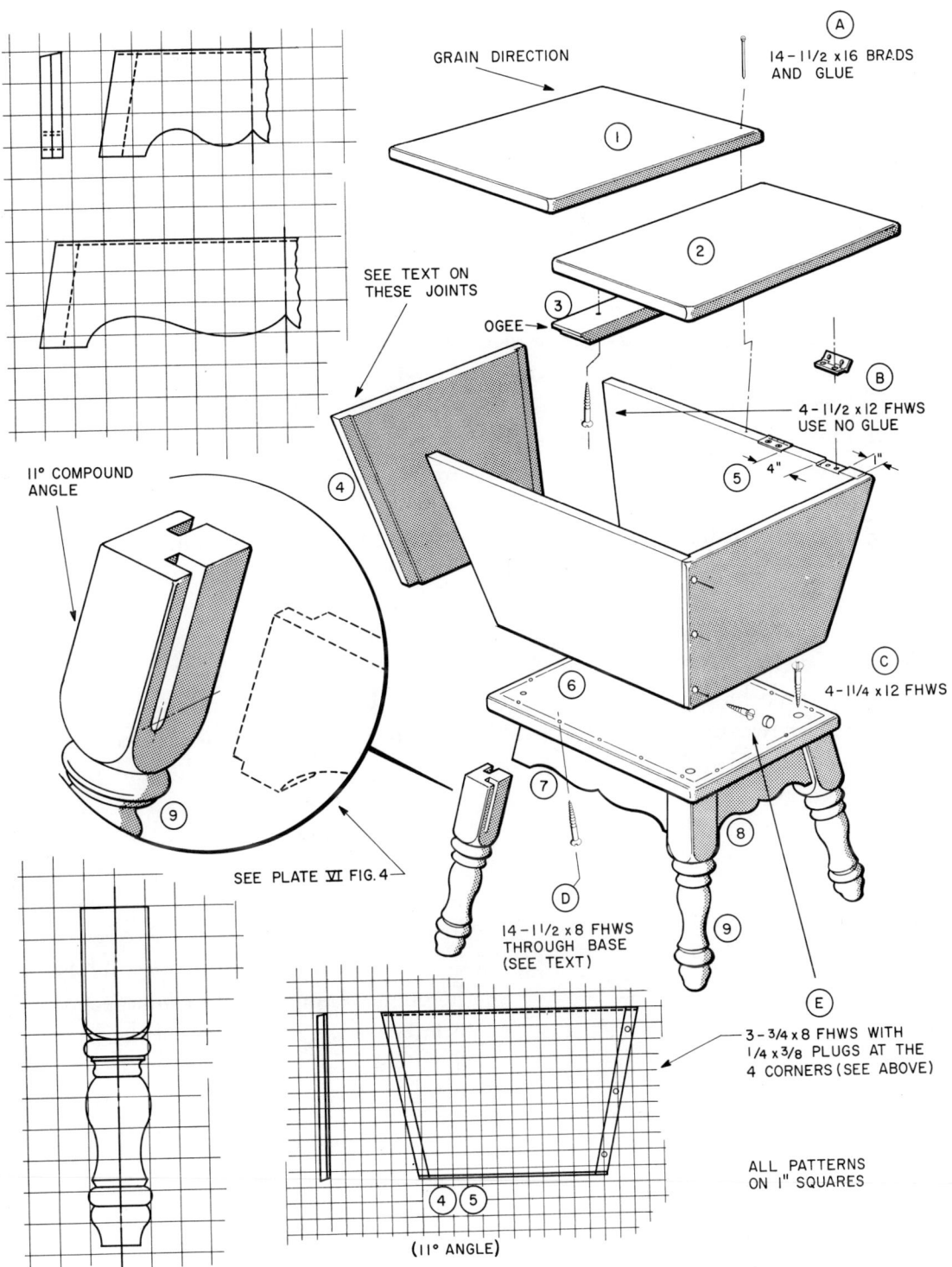

21. Dough Box End Table

22. Dry Sink

CURRENTLY the dry sink is one of the most popular favorites among colonial furniture enthusiasts. There are many possible variations in construction and arrangement of drawers and doors.

The piece illustrated is of medium size and may be placed easily in different areas of most rooms. A wide range of accessories aid in making the piece most effective and interesting. This particular sink has generous storage space within two drawers and a two door center section.

CONSTRUCTION NOTES

The main construction centers around the end panels and the door frame made up of stiles and rails that are shown as butt joints. For a more authentic joint see the drawing of the dry sink hutch for dovetailed stiles.

The drawer runners are somewhat different than those shown in Plate IV and are merely strips (10, 22) that are bradded into a partition (7 or 20) below it. (Use no glue to allow for possible adjustment should shrinkage occur.)

The 10° angle of the end piece should be carefully cut for a clean fit with the front panel. A separate jointed and grain matched piece may be glued to the end to make up this triangular area.

The front panel (16) should be thoroughly rounded in the center section to indicate wear. Also round the front and right side of the top piece (3), as well as the rear skirt, especially at the corners.

Dry Sink

Bill of Materials

PART	QUANTITY	DESCRIPTION	DIMENSION
1	1	Rear Skirt	3/4 x 4 1/2 x 35 1/4
2	2	End Skirts	3/4 x 2 1/2 x 8
3	1	Top	1 x 16 1/2 x 16
4	1	Rear Skirt Base	1 x 1 1/2 x 20 3/8
5	1	Back Panel	1/4 x 35 1/4 x 29 1/2
6	1	Right End Trim	3/4 x 1 x 15 3/8
7	1	Upper Partition	3/4 x 13 7/8 x 35 1/4
8	1	Main Divider	3/4 x 4 5/8 x 14 7/8
9	1	Sub Divider	1 x 2 x 4 5/8
10, 22	2	Drawer Runners	3/4 x 11/16 x 13 1/2
11	1	Upper Drawer Rail	5/8 x 1 x 9 3/4
12	2	Ends	3/4 x 14 1/4 x 32
13	1	Upper Left Stile	3/4 x 2 x 4 5/8
14	2	Main Stiles	3/4 x 2 x 25 3/8
15	1	Upper Main Rail	3/4 x 2 x 36
16	1	Front Panel	3/4 x 5 7/8 x 20 3/4
17	1	Center Stile	3/4 x 3 x 15 1/2
18	1	Center Partition	3/4 x 13 7/8 x 35 1/4
19	1	Center Partition Rail	3/4 x 1 x 32
20	1	Lower Partition	3/4 x 13 7/8 x 35 1/4
21	1	Lower Partition Rail	3/4 x 1 x 32
23	1	Front Base	3/4 x 4 3/4 x 38
24	2	End Bases	3/4 x 4 3/4 x 16
25	2	Upper Door Rails	3/4 x 2 1/2 x 11 5/8
26	4	Door Stiles	3/4 x 2 1/2 x 15 1/4
27	2	Lower Door Rails	3/4 x 2 5/8 x 11 5/8
28	2	Raised Door Panels	1/2 x 10 1/8 x 10 1/2
A	8	Brads	1 1/2 x 18
B	12	Brads	1 1/2 x 18
C	3	Brads	1 x 18
D	4	Brads	1 1/2 x 18
E	14	Brads	1 x 18
F	4	Flat Head Wood Screws	1 1/4 x 8
G	12	Brads	1 1/2 x 18
H	4	Flat Head Wood Screws	1 1/4 x 8
I	8	Brads	1 x 18
J	6	Flat Head Wood Screws	1 1/4 x 8
K	2	Porcelain Knobs	1 dia. (large drawer)
L	1	Porcelain Knob	3/4 dia.
M	2 pair	H Hinges	3
N	1 pair	H Latches	3

Dry Sink

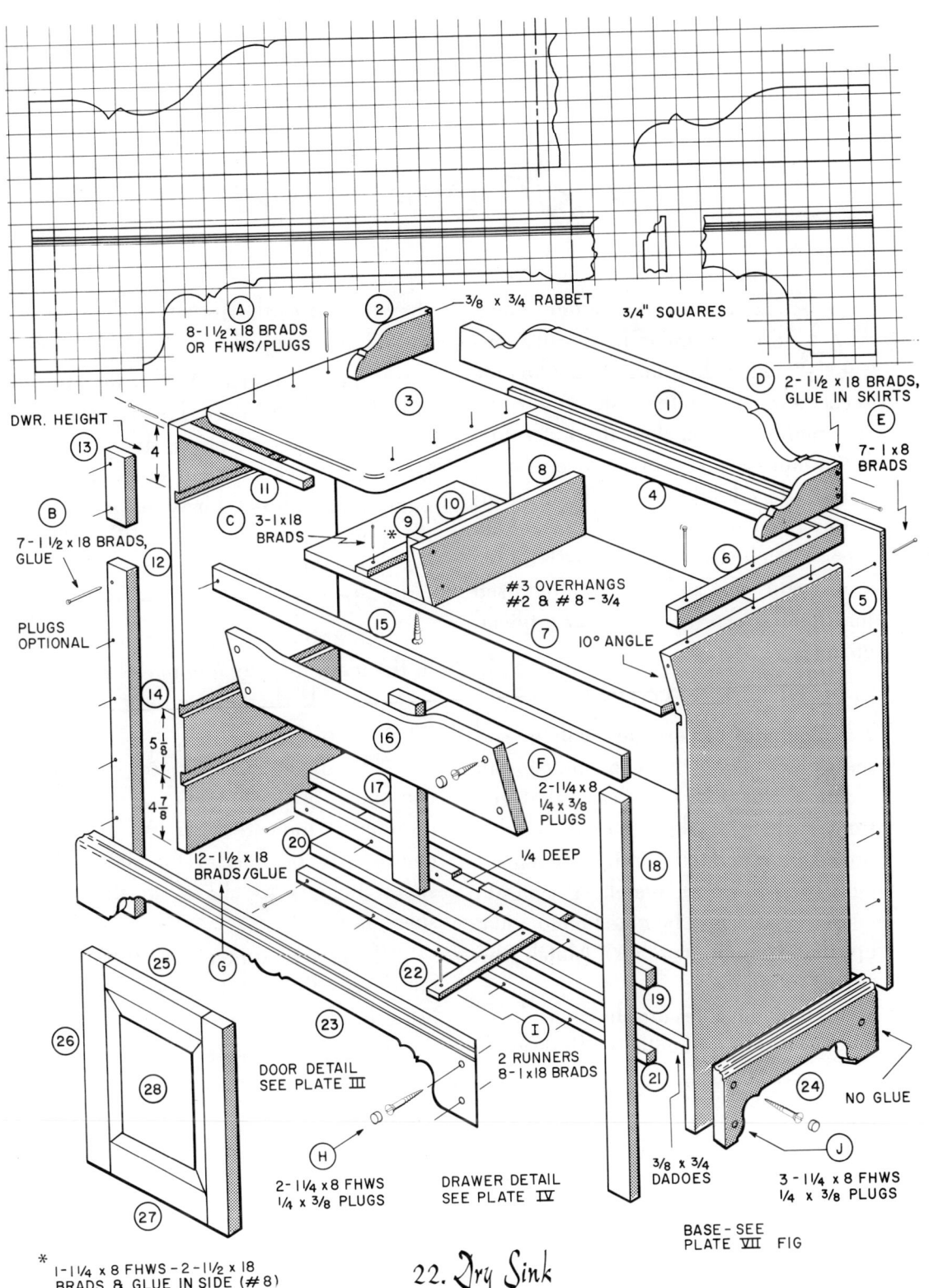

22. Dry Sink

23. Dry Sink Hutch

AN EXCELLENT combination piece, this is similar to the dry sink preceding and it also has top sections much like the hutch following. It is more informal than the hutch and has a more rugged appearance. It need not be placed only in the dining room; it has been used effectively in certain types of kitchens. Storage space is ample and useful. The sink area is often used for abundant sprays of real or artificial greenery.

CONSTRUCTION NOTES

Begin the construction with the end pieces (2). Brad them together to cut identical shapes. Take care that the front surface of the 15 degree angle projection is perfectly straight for a good joint with the front panel. A separate jointed piece could be glued on to make up this triangular areas. Match the grain.

The main stiles are shown as dovetail joints for authenticity. If desired, they can be shortened and simply butted, or dowelled.

Drawer runner (11) is merely a strip bradded in place. Use no glue so adjustment can be made should there be a shrinkage problem of drawer or panels. Thumb tacks may be placed in the upper main partition (17) under the lower edges of the drawer sides to reduce friction.

Care should be taken to accurately fit the main top (8) into place with the end piece. It should overhang ¾" on three sides.

The spoon rack is made with one continuous open slot and should be well rounded to indicate wear. An optional choice may be that of the individual spoon holders as shown in the wall spoon rack.

If the rear center skirt (18) does not draw tightly against the rear panel using brads, then two or three ¾" x 8 wood screws may help.

Dry Sink Hutch

Bill of Materials

PART	QUANTITY	DESCRIPTION	DIMENSION
1	1	Upper Skirt	3/4 x 7 3/8 x 35 1/2
2	2	Ends	3/4 x 13 3/4 x 55 1/4
3	1	Top Shelf	3/4 x 7 x 35 1/2
4	3	Drawer Dividers	3/4 x 4 1/2 x 7
5	1	Lower Drawer Shelf	3/4 x 7 x 35 1/2
6	1	Back Panel	1/4 x 35 1/2 x 47 1/2
7	1	Spoon Rack	3/4 x 3 3/4 x 34 3/4
8	1	Main Top	1 1/8 x 15 3/4 x 16
9	1	Upper Drawer Rail	1/2 x 3/4 x 9 7/8
10	1	Upper Right Stile	3/4 x 1 x 4 1/2
11	1	Drawer Runner	5/16 x 11/16 x 13 1/4
12	1	Upper Left Stile	3/4 x 1 1/2 x 4 1/2
13	2	Stiles	3/4 x 2 7/8 x 25 1/4
14	1	Upper Rail	3/4 x 1 3/4 x 36 1/4
15	1	Divider	3/4 x 4 1/2 x 14 1/2
16	1	Front Panel	3/4 x 4 7/8 x 21 3/4
17	1	Upper Main Partition	3/4 x 13 1/4 x 35 1/2
18	1	Rear Center Skirt	3/4 x 4 1/2 x 20 5/8
19	1	Center Stile	3/4 x 4 3/8 x 22
20	1	Center Shelf	3/4 x 13 1/4 x 35 1/2
21	1	Bottom	3/4 x 13 1/4 x 35 1/2
22	2	Bottom Rails	3/4 x 3/4 x 13 1/16
23	1	Front Base	3/4 x 5 1/4 x 37 3/4
24	2	End Bases	3/4 x 5 1/4 x 14 1/2
25	4	Door Rails	3/4 x 3 1/8 x 10 1/4
26	4	Door Stiles	3/4 x 2 7/8 x 18 7/8
27	2	Raised Door Panels	1/2 x 8 x 13 3/8
A	4	Flat Head Wood Screws	1 1/4 x 8
B	4	Brads	1 1/4 x 18
C	16	Brads	1 x 18
D	5	Flat Head Wood Screws	1 1/2 x 8
E	4	Brads	1 x 18
F	5	Brads	1 1/2 x 18
G	20	Flat Head Wood Screws	1 1/4 x 8
H	14	Brads	1 1/2 x 18
I	6	Flat Head Wood Screws	1 1/4 x 8
J	5	Porcelain Knobs	7/8 dia.
K	2 pair	H-L Hinges	3
L	2	H-Latches	3

Dry Sink Hutch

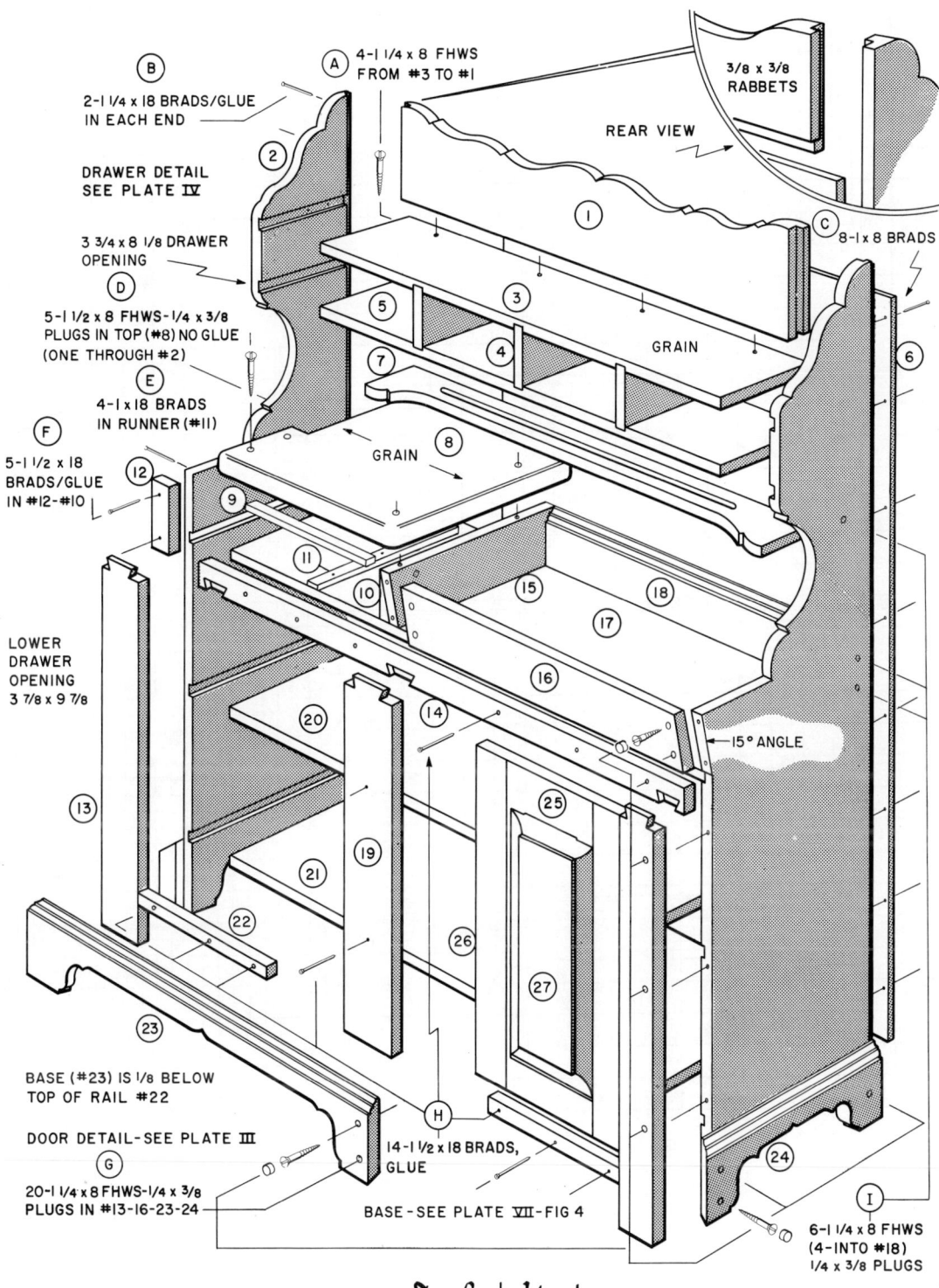

23a. Dry Sink Hutch

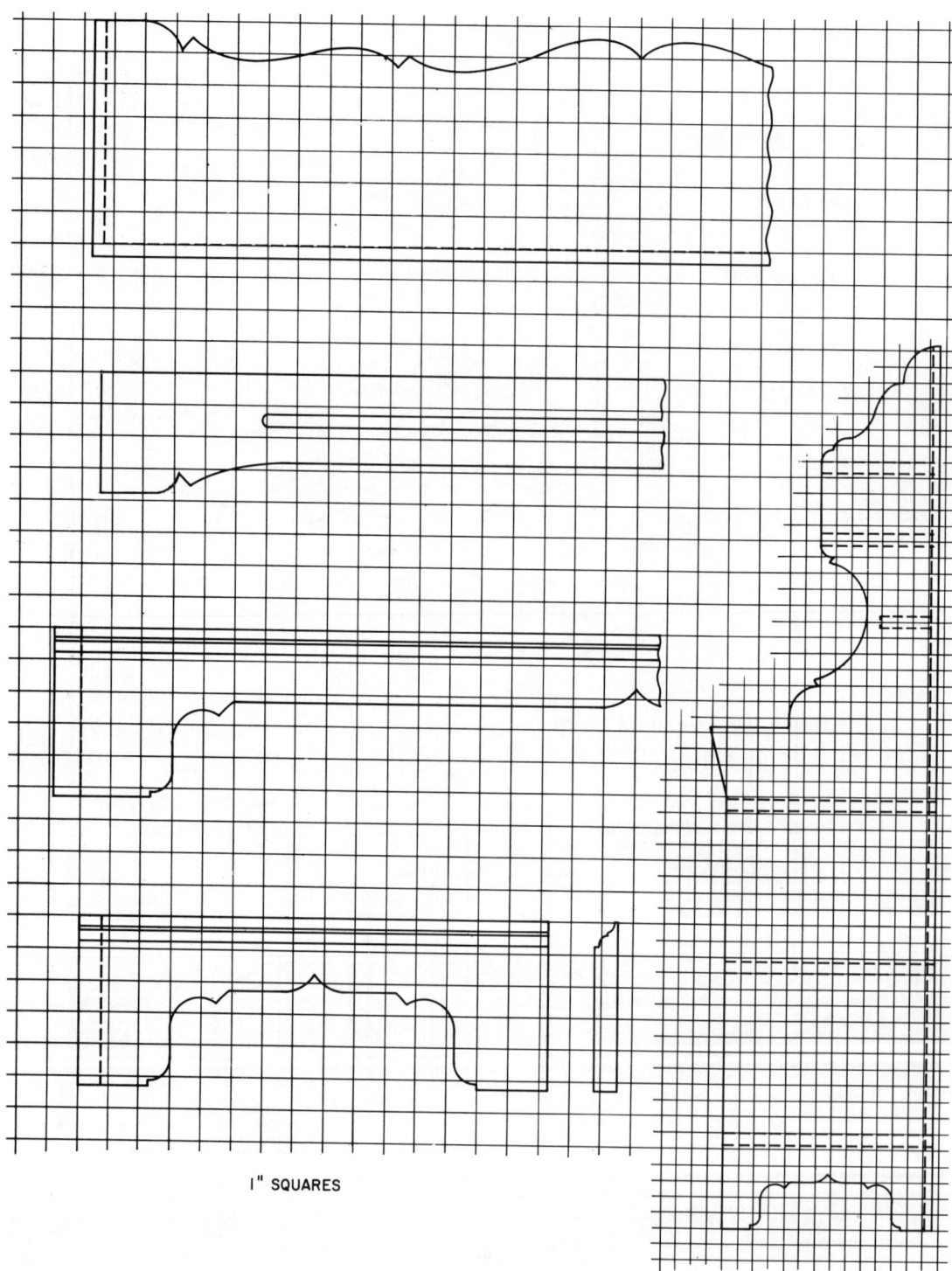

1" SQUARES

236. Dry Sink Hutch Patterns

24. Hutch

THIS HUTCH was chosen as an excellent example of proportion and design that makes it a fine piece of furniture for the average size home. It is not so massive that it cannot be placed in most dining room areas. The storage space is ample for an effective visual display as well as out-of-the-way storage of china, silverware, table linen and accessories.

CONSTRUCTION NOTES

The hutch is made up of two separate sections, the base and the hutch top. These are shown on separate plates.

24A. HUTCH BASE

The main stiles and rails of the base are shown with dovetail joints that give the authentic effect of colonial joinery. If desired, these parts may be shortened to make simple butt joints. Another option may be that of adding a center shelf for additional space for china storage.

The drawer runners (8) are different than those shown in Plate IV. They are merely strips bradded without glue directly to the upper shelf, (11). To make the drawers slide more easily, place four thumb tacks in the upper shelf (11) under the lower edges of the drawer sides to reduce friction. Bury them almost flush with the shelf. See Plate 1, Fig. 2 for drawer stops.

The top of the base unit may be molded as suggested in the view at the upper left in Plate I or similar cutter bits could be used.

24B. HUTCH TOP

Lightly brad the two end pieces (13) together before cutting so as to have duplicate shapes. The main shelves in the upper section are shown as glue joints only. An optional choice can be screws with plugs. The upper section is not fastened to the lower section but is held only by its own weight.

The crown moulding shown in the drawing is suggested. There are various other appropriate shapes.

The dentil (4, 5) (if not purchased) can be most easily cut on a radial or table saw. The dentils are mitered at the corners and should be glued only at the miter to allow for expansion of the ends.

The plate groove in the shelves are for standard dinner plate size. For smaller plates the groove should be moved back to about $1\frac{7}{8}''$ from rear edge.

The end pieces should be $1\frac{1}{8}''$ thick, as $\frac{3}{4}''$ stock is rather thin for strength and proper proportions. Thinner stock should be substituted only if absolutely necessary.

The lower skirt (14) is drawn tight against the back panel with wood screws (G) rather than brads. Screws may also be needed to draw the crown moulding (2, 3) into place tightly if the finishing nails are not enough for a clean snug joint line.

"Distress" all brad holes so they will be hidden from view when the hutch is stained and finished. See Section 3, Step 2.

See Section 4 for hardware.

Bill of Materials

PART	QUANTITY	DESCRIPTION	DIMENSION
1	1	Top	1 1/8 x 14 7/8 x 36
2	2	Cleats	3/4 x 1 x 11 1/4
3	1	Back Panel	1/4 x 33 1/2 x 31
4	2	Ends	3/4 x 13 1/4 x 31
5	1	Top Rail (inner)	1 x 1 1/2 x 32 3/4
6	1	Top Rail (outer)	3/4 x 1 x 31
7	2	Outer Stiles	3/4 x 2 3/8 x 31
8	2	Drawer Runners	5/16 x 11/16 x 12 7/8
9	2	Drawer Rails	3/4 x 1 x 14 3/4
10	1	Center Stile	3/4 x 3 x 28 1/2
11	1	Upper Shelf	3/4 x 12 7/8 x 33 1/2
12	1	Bottom Shelf	3/4 x 12 7/8 x 33 1/2
13	2	Lower Rails	3/4 x 3/4 x 14 3/4
14	2	End Bases	3/4 x 5 1/2 x 14 7/8
15	1	Front Base	3/4 x 5 1/2 x 35 3/4
16	2	Upper Door Rails	3/4 x 2 1/2 x 10 3/4
17	2	Lower Door Rails	3/4 x 2 3/4 x 10 3/4
18	4	Door Stiles	3/4 x 2 1/4 x 19 3/8
19	2	Raised Door Panels	1/2 x 9 1/2 x 14 7/8
A	10	Flat Head Wood Screws	1 1/4 x 10
B	4	Flat Head Wood Screws	1 3/4 x 10
C	12	Brads	1 x 18
D	8	Brads	1 x 18
E	2	Flat Head Wood Screws	1 1/4 x 8
F	6	Flat Head Wood Screws	1 1/4 x 8
G	24	Brads	1 1/2 x 18
H	11	Flat Head Wood Screws	1 1/4 x 8
I	2	Porcelain Knobs	1 dia.
J	2 pair	H L Hinges	3
K	1 pair	H Latches	3

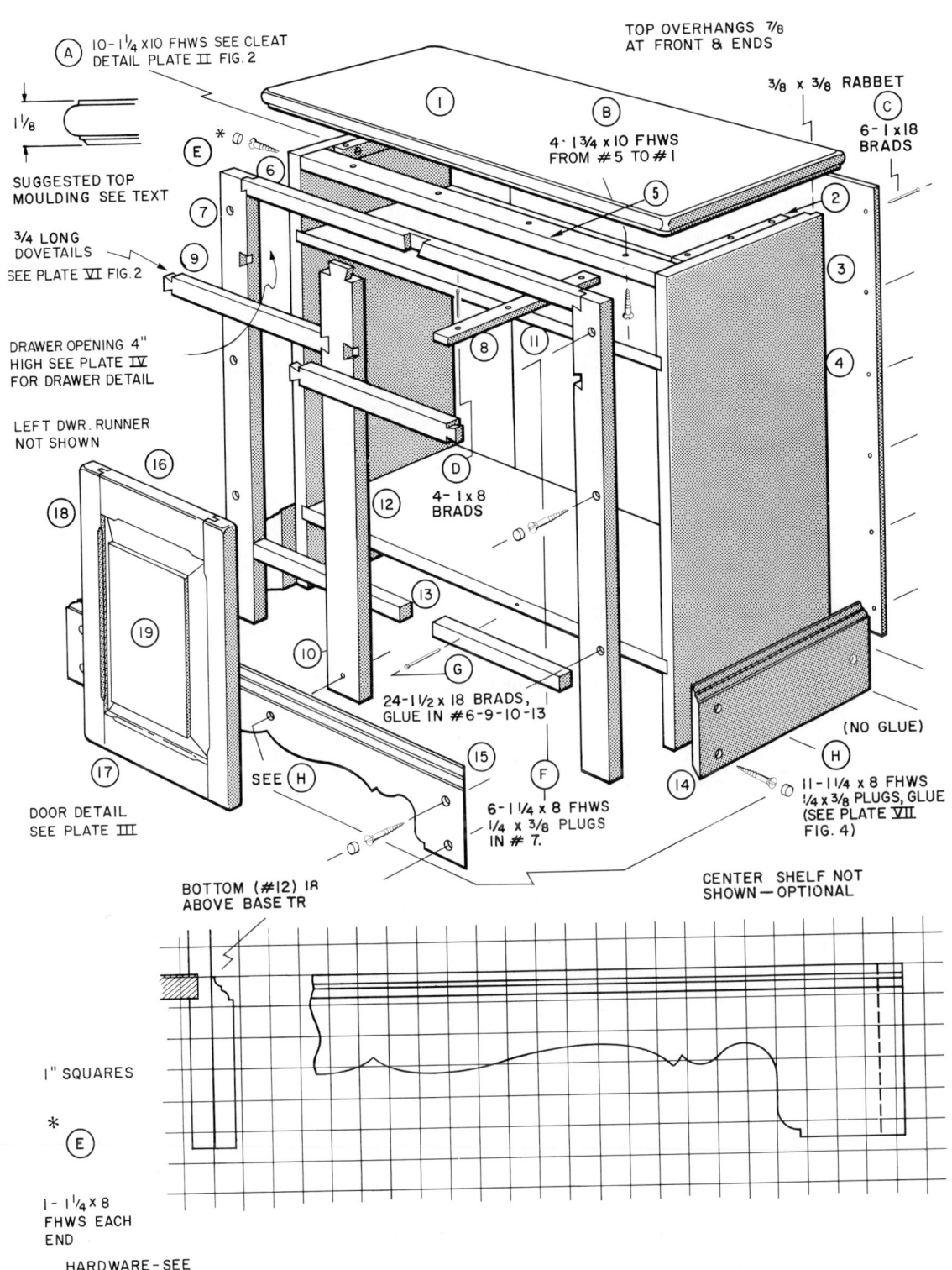

24a. Hutch Base

Bill of Materials

PART	QUANTITY	DESCRIPTION	DIMENSION
1	1	Top	3/4 x 7 7/8 x 32 1/8
2	2	End Crown Mouldings	2 x 2 x 11 3/4
3	1	Front Crown Mouldings	2 x 2 x 38 1/4
4	2	End Dentils	1/4 x 1 5/8 x 10
5	1	Front Dentil	1/4 x 1 5/8 x 34 1/2
6	1	Upper Skirt	*1 1/8 x 3 1/4 x 33 5/8
7	1	Back Panel	1/4 x 32 1/8 x 38 pine plywood
8	1	Top Shelf	3/4 x 8 1/8 x 32 1/8
9	1	Top Shelf Skirt	1/2 x 1 1/2 x 31 3/8
10	1	Plate Shelf	3/4 x 9 1/8 x 32 1/8
11	3	Drawer Dividers	3/4 x 4 1/4 x 9 1/8
12	1	Drawer Shelf	3/4 x 9 1/8 x 32 1/8
13	2	Ends	*1 1/8 x 9 1/2 x 38
14	1	Lower Skirt	3/4 x 4 5/8 x 31 3/8
15	1	Lower Skirt Moulding	7/16 x 7/16 x 31 3/8
16	2	Interior End Mouldings	7/16 x 7/16 x 9 3/4
17	2	Front End Mouldings	7/16 x 7/16 x 2 1/4
18	2	Outside End Mouldings	7/16 x 7/16 x 10
A	14	Finishing Nails	1 3/4 (5d)
B	4	Finishing Nails	1 3/4 (5d)
C	14	Brads	3/4 x 18
D	36	Brads	1 x 18
E	8	Brads	1 1/2 x 18
F	21	Brads	3/4 x 18
G	4	Flat Head Wood Screws	3/4 x 8
H	4	Flat Head Wood Screws	1 1/2 x 8
I	4	Porcelain Knobs	3/4 dia.

* 1 1/8 Recommended — 7/8 Acceptable

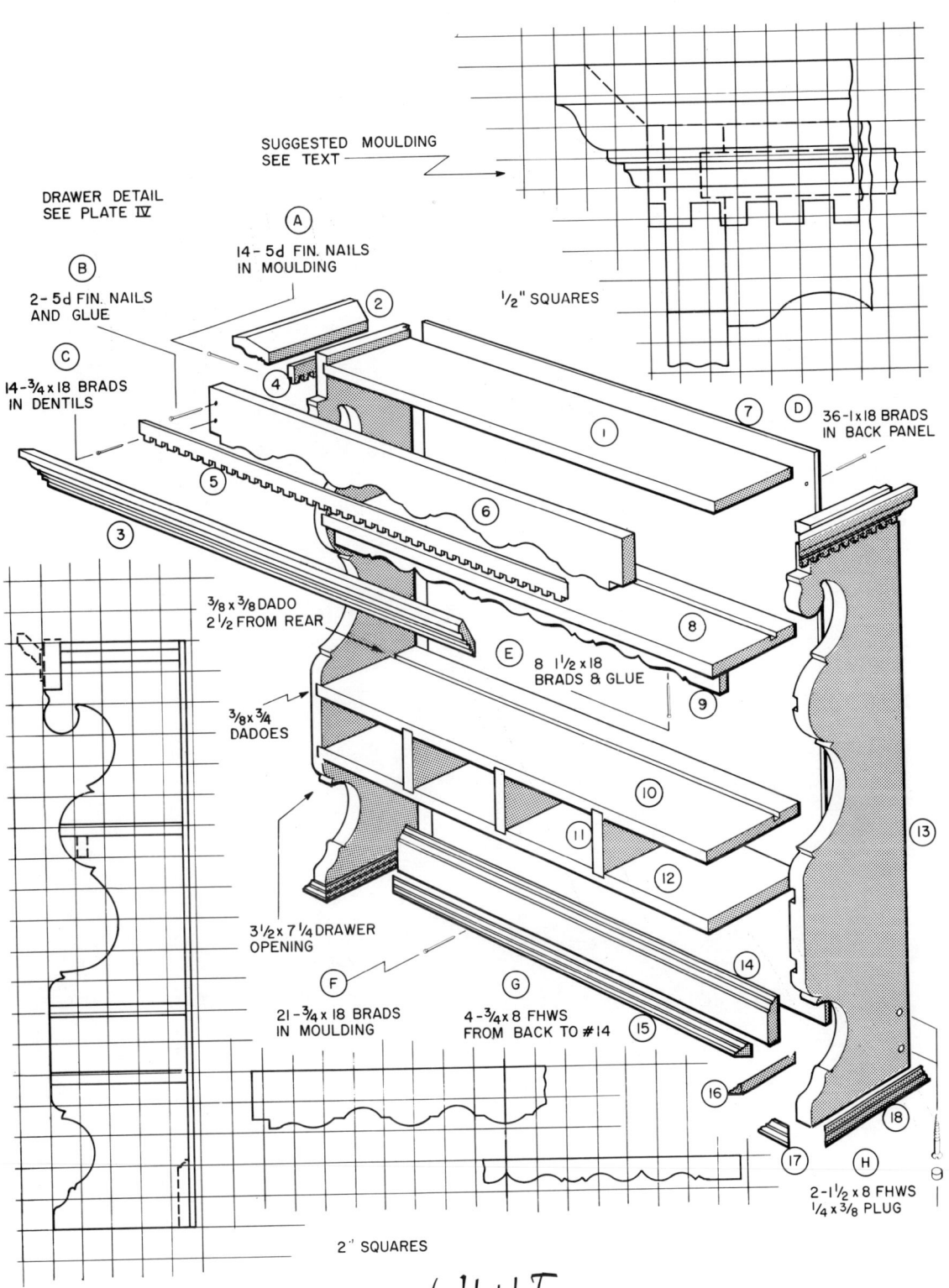

246. Hutch Top